Cliff Parker has written, humorously, on the subject of fishing for many years. His bestselling *The Fishing Handbook to End All Fishing Handbooks* is also available in Sphere. Cliff Parker now writes for the *TV Times*.

Hook, Line and Stinker

CLIFF PARKER

SPHERE BOOKS LIMITED
30–32 Gray's Inn Road, London WC1X 8JL

First published in Great Britain by
Wolfe Publishing Limited 1975
Copyright © Cliff Parker 1975
Published by Sphere Books Ltd 1983

Reproduced, printed and bound in Great Britain by
Hazell Watson & Viney Ltd, Aylesbury, Bucks

Serious Bit

This book is based on the best (or worst—you can't please 'em all) of my weekly pieces in *Angling Times*. My thanks are due to *AT* for all the help, encouragement and space they gave me.

Thanks, too, to all the lovely people.

To the family: Dearly Beloved, Number One Son, Darling Daughter and Daft Cat. Who have to put up with it all.

To the mates: Mad Mac, Big McGinty and Irish Patrick. Up with whom I have to put.

And to all the scruffy, smelly, screwball anglers whose saga this is. God bless us. Every one.

Cliff Parker

Contents

(continued overleaf)

Introduction

What is there to say that has not been said a thousand times already?
   Nothing.
   All right then.
   I'll shut up.

Cliff Parker

Welcome to our world

Every season sees several thousand (put your teeth in to say that) keen young lads about to take up the rod seriously for the first time.

Welcome to our world. But make sure you know what you're letting yourself in for. Anglers, you see, are not normal people.

Now, when I say not normal, I don't mean not *normal*. I mean not . . . er, what's the word? Normal.

Anglers are, for a start, and to put no finer point on it, scruffy. You can't fish in a Savile Row suit. And you tend to get fond of the clothes you fish in, and not want to part with them. Or have them washed or cleaned or anything poncy like that.

If this happens, if the wife grabs the lot when you're not looking and tubs it, you find all the pockets full of pulped club permits, curly quills, and dead maggots ironed out to the size of a 10p piece.

What's worse, all your clobber will have gone back into shape. And it won't fit anywhere, because years of carrying a heavy basket and sitting huddled up on freezing mornings will have put *you* well and truly out of shape.

Anglers tend to pong. Apart from the ancient clothes and the things you tend to step in when you're crossing a field, there are lots of extra pong-provoking agents like mummified maggots, chunks of old cheese and layers of fish slime, none of which smell exactly like Chanel No. 5.

There was the sad case of the shortsighted angler who lost his cap in a cow pasture. He tried on fifty before he found his own.

(Another thing you'll have to put up with is revolting jokes like that.)

. . . So you may find your social life a bit restricted. Only other anglers can bear the company of a scruffy, smelly, grubby, unshaven heap. If you fancy yourself as a bit of a lad with the girls, forget it. The approach of what looks like a five-foot-nine caddis grub with lustful intentions is enough to send any girl screaming into the night for the nearest paddy waggon.

If a girl is misguided enough, or shortsighted enough, to marry an angler, she never again finds time hanging heavily. She is occupied with a thousand delightful little jobs like cutting the grass,

papering the walls, mending the fuses and doing the odd spot of bricklaying, pausing only now and again to look at a photograph of her beloved to remind her of what he looks like.

She has problems with the children, too. When the old man does finally stumble in after a weekend's fishing, how does she answer the kids' question of, 'Who's that funny man, mummy?'

If she comes clean and says, 'That's your daddy, darlings', she runs the risk of giving the poor little perishers a complex for life.

Your social life will have other problems which we shall discuss in the next chapter. Meanwhile, this is our world . . . and welcome to it.

When somebody thinks you're 'orrible

You have been apprised already of certain social disabilities inseparable from the Noble Art. (That's another one never to say with your teeth out.) There are a great many other inconveniences, occasioned by the fact that certain categories of people do not love anglers one little bit.

Bank managers do not love anglers. They just cannot understand why the reasons for an overdraft should include bent swingtips, lost floats, gunjed-up reels and the spending of hard earned cash on fifteen gallons of maggots, twenty-five loaves, four pounds of cheese and a hundredweight of bran. All of which has been chucked in the river.

Insurance men do not love anglers. Claim forms on personal accident policies include such improbable horrors as rod rests up noses, lead weights in earholes and treble hooks in the strangest places. This means another trip up to Head Office to explain the whole thing and another sherracking from the Area Manager for issuing policies to such maniacs in the first place.

Publicans do not love anglers. In spite of the fact that without them their takings would be halved overnight. They don't mind anglers handing over lots of lovely money, but they do object to them standing around the bar, making the place look untidy and putting the other customers off their ale.

Doctors do not love anglers. Apart from wanting sick notes whenever the weather looks promising, they keep coming in with strange complaints like congestion of the gills, lumbago of the lateral line, frayed webbing between the toes and cowpat poisoning. Doctors who really know their stuff just wrap up the anglers in brown paper and post them off to the Natural History Museum.

Hairdressers do not love anglers. Instead of going in once a fortnight for a shampoo, trim, blow wave and manicure, they tromp in once a year looking like orphaned yetis and demand a threepenny all-off.

Bosses do not love anglers. They find that on mild days, especially early in the season, there is a suspiciously high incidence of bad backs and dead grandmas. They are not keen on the way anglers crawl into work on Monday, coughing, and sit there all day with their eyes shut.

Restaurateurs do not love anglers. Restaurateurs, in fact, do not let them in, either on the grounds that they are not wearing ties or simply in the interests of public hygiene.

Café proprietors do not love anglers. As Monsieur Basil, of Basil's Caff, said only the other day, 'Well, it puts the regular clientele orf, dunnit? When a bloke's 'ad 'ard day dahn the coke yard, 'e don't want ter come in 'ere and 'ave ter sit wiv a bunch o' scruffs, do 'e?'

Bus conductors do not love anglers. It puts a great strain on one's ideals of working class solidarity to be greeted with: 'Yer can't tek that lot on 'ere, Jack. What d'yer think this is—bloody Pickfords? An' Ah'm not ringin' this bell until yer off.'

Mothers-in-law do not love anglers. For the way they treat their daughters. But mothers-in-law do not love anybody, anyway, so you're on to a hiding to nothing there.

*　　*　　*

So there you are, lads. Take up angling and you will find yourself ostracised by society, permanently broke, under-insured and totally unloved. But up with all this you will cheerfully put, for the compensations that this ancient and noble pastime brings. Compensations such as . . . such as . . . er . . . such as . . .

What I mean is, you can't have everything, can you?

Ready, steady . . . just a minute

All set for the start of the season, lads, are you?

Sure? I don't want to worry you, but it might be worth checking through your gear. Things happen to it in the close season.

You've got your club cards. Of course you haven't. For three months you've been meaning to write off for them next week.

Your anorak, ganzi and bobbly hat. They've not been passed on to Oxfam or quietly incinerated, have they? The missus didn't shell out a bob to a passing Boy Scout to take them away and have them put down, did she?

Titter ye not. I know more than one lad who has had to buy back his rig from the local jumble sale, beating off farmers who were looking for something special for the scarecrow.

Your wicker basket isn't in the props department of Darling Daughter's school drama society, is it?

The baiting needle. Didn't the school drama society run up some things in sacking for the spear carriers in *Antigone Meets The Wolf Man*, and wasn't Miss Pringle asking the kids if they had a needle big enough to take some thick string?

The bait tins. Did you really empty them and scald them out after your last trip? Or are they now lying about like whited sepulchres, full of 'orrible dead buzzers? Worse than that, full of 'orrible live buzzers?

The rods. You hung them carefully in their cases, as it tells you to in *Angling For Idiots*. If you didn't, if they have been lying for three months in the shed under a pile of crates and old newspapers, do not despair. You can give them to the school drama society for Christmas. They're always short of shepherds' crooks for the Nativity play.

The pike gag. Remember your lad asking if you had anything he could use to get the tyre off his bike? And remember telling him to go and flaming well look, instead of pestering you all the time? Might be worth asking him, ever so kindly, whether he put it back.

The rod rests. And the time old Fred came over with his kids. His kids and your kids, playing happily in the back. First at cricket, for which they were needing some stumps. Secondly at Olympic javelin throwing. Gives you an uneasy feeling, doesn't it? That your rod rests might having gone sailing over the back to stick quivering in Jim-next-door's jungle of a shrubbery. To have stayed there all this time. Gently rusting.

The reels. You did take the line off, strip them down, clean them

and oil them. Or did you perhaps leave them jumbled in a wet plastic bag, nestling together in a bed of coarse river sand? Check now, if you like, by giving one of them a quick turn. If you get a *clunk-click-errrrrrrccccccchhhhhhh*, you've been a naughty lad and it might cost you a bob or two.

Almost forgot the wellies. It would not be like you to leave them in the shed with the seaboot stockings still inside, would it? If you did, you will now be faced with the heartrending task of evicting two families. Of little mice. If your humanitarian principles are too strong, or if you are scared of mice, don't attempt it. Send the wife.

*　　　*　　　*

On the first day of the season, if you find yourself ticketless, clobberless and gearless, don't sit at home fretting. Go down to the canal and watch the other lads enjoying themselves. You'll find other forgetful lads like yourself, with nothing to do but stand and swear. I've got a nasty feeling that one of them might be me.

14

Will you be my Valentine?

Strange, isn't it, that although lots of people write about angling, though the sport has a vast prose literature, you never find the poets getting carried away by it. And nobody sings songs about it.

'It's not romantic, that's why,' said Dearly Beloved. 'Nobody's going to get lyrical over a bunch of scruffs who sit around all day drowning worms.'

That's where she's wrong. I have got lyrical. And for St Valentine's Day. You can't get much more romantic than that.

You will shortly be reading the Parker Anthology of Angling Valentines. It's all free, lads. If you want to use any of them to slay the girl of your dreams—or even the wife—just pick where you like.

> *I was looking at my float a-bobbing,*
> *When my stricken heart began a-throbbing;*
> *Thinking of you, you gorgeous dish—*
> *And that's how I missed the flaming fish.*

Not bad for a start, was it? Or perhaps you'd prefer something deeper and more sophisticated. How about:

> *Whenever I catch a big fat chub,*
> *Or when I find myself in the club,*
> *   I think of you, dear, I think of you.*
>
> *When a perch puts its fin up, all a-bristle,*
> *Or the steward blows the final whistle,*
> *   I think of you, dear, I think of you.*
>
> *When a chill wind blows in from the south*
> *Or a pike opens up its great big mouth,*
> *   I think of you, dear, I think of you.*

Perhaps not. Something a bit sexier?

> *My nose is like a red, red rose,*
> *That's newly sprung in June.*
> *It's caused by standing in the wind*
> *And fishing with a spoon.*
> *Standing there, I sometimes drool,*
> *And then I start to pine.*
> *Instead of spooning for the ice-cold fish,*
> *I could spoon with you, Valentine.*

The musical lads could try this one, sung to the tune of *You're the Cream in My Coffee*:

> *You're the swing in my swingtip.*
> *You're the shot on my line.*
> *You're my crusty flake.*
> *You're my cocoa break.*
> *You're my Va-ha-lentine.**

Here's one for the domesticated lads:

> *Though the bobbly hat you knitted*
> *Makes me look like a garden gnome;*
> *Though you moan about the maggots in the freezer;*
> *Though the pullover from your mother*
> *Trips me up whenever I move,*
> *And the lads think I'm a very henpecked geezer;*
> *Though I've got to leave my wellies*
> *In the garden with the worms;*
> *Though my keepnet can't hang on your washing line;*
> *And you'll only touch my fishing socks*
> *With the end of a garden pole;*
> *Missis, will you be my Valentine?*

For those of us, brethren, who occasionally stray from the paths of righteousness on the way home, how about:

> *Though the art of fishing I haven't yet mastered;*
> *Though I stay out late and come home plastered;*
> *Please believe me when I say,*
> *I love you on St Valentine's Day.*

If that doesn't melt her heart, there's only one thing left to say:

> *Rudd fins are red.*
> *Tench fins are green.*
> *Please put me down*
> *'Til you know where I've been.*

---

* It has to be Va-ha-lentine to fit the no-ho-ho-hotes.

Cousin Jim and the big hairy brown thing

Cousin Jim from Leeds and I were sitting side by side on the banks of the Swale. Talking about this, that and the other (in roughly equal proportions). When this big hairy brown thing crashed right down between us and knocked us off our baskets.

I was a bit dazed for a minute. It's not every day that big hairy brown things fall on me. I think Cousin Jim was a bit dazed, too, because only his wellies were sticking out from under it.

'What the bloody 'ell is it?' he croaked, a bit muffled because it's difficult to speak with your mouth full.

The big hairy brown thing went, 'Mooo . . .'

'It's a cow,' I said. Quick as a flash.

'Well get the bloody thing off me 'ead.'

'Right! On yer feet! Hup, hup, hup! MOVE!!!,' I yelled in my nastiest corporal's voice.

It did it. Funny, that, because none of the lads used to take any notice. ('Make yer bed, Ernie,' I said to Driver Newbold on the morning of the Major General's inspection. 'Go on, just for me.')

The cow stood there, looking confused. Cousin Jim lay there, looking squashed. What had happened was that the cow had grazed right to the edge of the undercut bank above us, and suddenly the ratio of weight of cow to depth of soil had turned critical.

'What we have to do, Jim,' I said, taking complete command of the situation, 'is to get this cow from down here to back up there.'

'It's facing the wrong way.'

'We just turn it round. I'll pull on this horn thing and you get hold of its tail and pull the other way.'

It worked beautifully. Except that the cow backheeled at the last minute and kicked Jim into the river.

'I'm getting a bit fed up with this,' he said.

'Patience, Jim lad. We're nearly there. If you'll just stop messing about in that water we can shove it to the top.'

We got the cow facing a sandy incline. Taking one haunch each, we both shoved and made noises like Frankie Laine. 'Yo! Hi! Yahee!' And that.

The cow gathered speed up the incline, so much so that my hand slipped and I fell down the bank. Cousin Jim, gallant lad, planted a hand on both haunches and gave a titanic final heave.

The cow scrambled over the top on to the turf. Whether out of exertion or relief we shall never know, but at the last second it lost control of its social graces and lifted its tail. Cousin Jim copped for the lot.

'Look what you've done!' he bawled. 'If you think I'm coming fishing with you again . . . '

'Now, Jim, it wasn't me. It was the cow. You've done a grand job. I'll buy you a pint.'

'You'll buy me six.'

'Done.'

The landlady passed over two pints, sniffed, and looked hard at Jim, who had tried to hide himself at a dark corner table.

'He with you?'

'Yes.'

'Well would he mind standing in the yard? He's stinking the place out.'

'Jim, would you mind standing in the yard? You're stinking the place out.'

'It's raining buckets out there.'

'Don't worry, Jim. I'll pass the pints through the window.'

What Jim said I cannot repeat. You can get locked up for that. Funny. He's normally such a quiet lad.

... being extracts from the diaries and other documents of the Sludgethorpe Waltonians. This from the diary of Horace Harris, the little quiet feller.

The trouble with Harry

Went down to Jackson's Clay Pit with Harry Turner. His ferret had a touch of the sniffles, so he brought it with him in his pocket to give it some fresh air.

There wasn't much fresh air in Harry's pocket, so the ferret kept sticking its head out for a sniff. Harry clouted it and it bit him.

After an hour my float bobbed and I was into a hard fighting roach which turned the scales at $1\frac{1}{2}$ oz, a personal record. Harry had drawn a blank, so he switched to cheese.

Half an hour later he had a bite, but struck late and lost his cheese. When he tried to re-bait, he found that the ferret had been out of his pocket and eaten his chunk of Sainsbury's Cheddar. He clouted the ferret and it bit him.

As the sun rose over the pit (I think it rose; it was hard to tell through the drizzle and the dust from the morning shift at the brickworks) we talked pleasantly of our dear ones. Harry's Vera's leg was troubling her again and young Jason had been expelled from Foundry Road Comprehensive for making suggestive remarks to the maths mistress. 'He's at that funny age,' said Harry.

Harry eventually took a perch on borrowed maggots. A handsome specimen, apart from its missing back fin. And in quick succession I took two lively young ($\frac{1}{4}$ oz) gudgeon.

Alas, the sun was rising higher; the traffic on the bypass behind the pit was getting heavier, and the ferret was getting restless. There would be no more fish that morning.

There was, however, an unexpected bonus. The ferret had come out for a sniff round my butty packet at the same time as a splendidly proportioned Muscovy duck. The duck pecked the ferret, which responded by pecking the duck. Dead.

'This will go nicely with some orange sauce,' said Harry, stuffing the duck into his basket.

'One moment, dear friend,' I said. 'They were my butties.'

'Oh, aye,' said Harry. 'But it was my bloody ferret.'

We packed up and walked down to *The Bricklayer's Arms*, a pleasant old world hostelry built about 1934. The public bar was renovated in 1953 and still retains the little coloured lights and plastic ivy.

Harry put his ferret on the counter. Experience had taught him that this often attracted the attention of visitors, who would express interest in the animal and buy him a drink. Harry, not the ferret.

The ferret began to eat the plateful of savoury cheese nibbles, placed there by a thoughtful management to titillate the palates of their customers. And increase their thirsts.

'Will you get that thing off my counter?' said Jolly Alice, the landlady, in a bantering tone. 'Before I flatten it.'

'You touch my faithful little ferret,' replied Harry, entering into the spirit of the repartee, 'and I will fetch you one across the black roots with this Muscovy duck.'

With a defiant chuckle, Jolly Alice clouted the ferret. The ferret bit her.

Everybody laughed. Except the ferret, Jolly Alice, and Alice's 17-stone husband. Mine host. Big Eddie. Who appeared from the saloon, jammed Harry's cap over his eyes and threw him through the door without opening it. He threw the ferret after him. The duck after the ferret. And myself after the duck.

That evening, Harry and I sat in the vault of *The Hangman's Noose*, not our favourite place of rest and refreshment, but one dictated for the moment by necessity. The Muscovy duck had been deposited with Harry's Vera, who was at that very moment looking through her Zena Skinner cookery book.

Harry and I reminisced over the events of the day. Marvelled at the beauties of the clay pit and the splendid fighting qualities of the fish. Laughed heartily and long over the antics of the ferret, Jolly Alice and Big Eddie.

Then the policeman came in. Looking, we heard him say to the barman, for a bloke with a ferret who had unlawfully come by a Muscovy duck and with it had caused a breach of the peace.

*   *   *

I called round at the station later. Harry was in Cell Three, pending certain enquiries. The desk sergeant let me take him in the plate covered in foil.

'Smells great,' said Harry. 'But that's the one trouble with ducks—never much on 'em.'

Future imperfect

I don't believe in horoscopes, you understand. Just read them for laughs. But this one was a goodie. For the weekend.

An eventful time ahead. Travel should be interesting. You will find plenty of scope for exercise under bracing conditions in the open air. You will make an intriguing new acquaintance, perhaps two or three. Sport is in the air. Interesting contact with a neighbour. A friend may turn up unexpectedly, counting on you for help and comfort.

Great, I thought. Let's get the rods out. Tip Number One Son from his pit before the first rosy fingers of dawn. Get with the travel, the exercise, the sport. Under God's clear sky. Could do with a quick brace. Discover the new acquaintance, have a happy neighbourly chat and comfort an old buddy.

The travel was highly interesting. The car stopped three miles from Leighton Buzzard and wouldn't shift. The exercise was exhilarating as we shoved the old thing a quarter of a mile to a garage. Where we waited until it opened up. And the skilled mechanic diagnosed a chronic lack of petrol.

We got the bracing conditions by courtesy of the freezing Nor'easter which blew up as soon as the rods were unpacked. Bringing with it a truly invigorating mix of hail and sleet. Oh, for the new acquaintance.

'Dad,' said Number One Son, wandering back from a bend upriver. 'There's a bloke down there who has just played hell with me and told me to thingy off. Says I'm fishing too close.'

'Well you just stay here, me old fruit. And take no notice.'

'Oh, no. I'm going back. Only came round for some more maggots. I'm a good forty yards away. And you could easily handle him, dad. He looks a right softy to me.'

Back he went. Five minutes later there was the sound of an intellectual voice shouting, 'Gerrarovit! Or I'll knock yer finging teef dahn yer finging froat!'

Gad, I thought. My firstborn is in need of me. Of his papa's strong right arm and killer punch. And mayhap the toe of the old wellie.

Round the bend was sitting Softy.

'That your mate?' he said. 'Tell him to gerroff aht of it or I'll etc., etc. . . . '

'Ho,' was my defiant replication. 'Will you?' Flexing my whipcord muscles and trying to remember how the killer punch worked.

'Yis,' he said. And stood up.

Ever met one of those blokes who stand up and keep on going?

'Son,' I called, 'let us leave this gentleman to his innocent recreation. Follow me.'

'Good job you did that, dad,' whispered Number One Son. 'He was a bit bigger than I thought. Mind you, he wasn't as rough-looking as his two mates down below that bank . . . '

The new acquaintances not having proved congenial, the sport being non-existent, and the open air a bit over-bracing, we went home.

There, back at the ranch house, I found plenty of groundbait left. A bit on the sloppy side, but it seemed a shame just to throw it away. So I did my St Francis bit. Threw it on top of the shed for the birds.

Either my aim was off or I hadn't allowed for the wind. The bait went over the shed, over the fence, and fell with a splat on what turned out to be the head of Irish Jim next door. Hi there, neighbour.

. . . Good job Jim is an understanding feller, I was saying to Dearly Beloved, when the phone rang. Mad Mac.

'Hello, ol' buddy,' he said in urgent tones. 'I have a small problem I should like to discuss. Can you make it in your motor-car to the *Queen and Cobbler*?'

I was there in ten minutes flat. Helping hand and wisdom beyond my years at the disposal of my old comrade. 'Two pints, please, landlord. Now, old buddy, what is troubling your poor little mind?'

'The lack,' said Mac, 'of ready cash. I'm skint. Can you lend me a fiver until next week?'

I should have stayed in bed.

Have I got the gear for you . . .

'Pater,' said Number One Son. (Great lad with the Latin, he is. It's bound to come in useful if ever he bumps into a Lat.) 'Pater, why is your name never on any fishing tackle? Why have you never invented anything? Why are not the tackle firms clamouring for your endorsement of their products?'

He knew, really, the lanky, hairy twit. He was just goading me. Taking the zombala. Getting up my little nose.

The reason, apart from my innate modesty and pathological shyness, is that everybody wants gear designed by the Top Angling Brains. Ivan Marks's floats. Fred J. Taylor's rods. Dick Walker's anything you care to mention.

But nobody wants gear designed by the Top Angling Idiot. It's sad, is that.

I've got it, mind you. Trunks full of plans, blueprints, specifications, ideas. Just to show Number One Son that his dad has more between the ears than a mush of classic proportions and breathtaking beauty, I am going to reveal details of inventions that hitherto have been cloaked in the utmost secrecy.

The Parker Prangproof Pogo Stick. For leaping over stiles and five-barred gates in one space-devouring bound. Its tripod legs with built-in shock absorbers ensure smooth and hernia-free landings.

The Parker Snughug Truss. For those who prefer to climb stiles in the old-fashioned way, but who are getting a bit apprehensive about the high kick at the top. Also for those who didn't quite get the hang of the Parker Prangproof Pogo Stick and whose landing was not quite as smooth and hernia-free as it might have been.

The Parker Swingalong Lightweight Telescopic Crutches. A neat aluminium pair, designed as insurance against pilot error in the use either of the Prangproof Pogo Stick or the Snughug Truss.

The Parker Perforated Early Warning Waders. These natty, thigh-length waders have a row of holes just above each kneecap. These let in water to warn you that you're going out of your depth, that the water's rising, or that the tide's coming in.

The Parker Blongwell Swan Dissuader. A short, stout, seasoned ash handle attacked to a length of chain, on the end of which is a 2-lb. iron ball studded with three-inch spikes. Awaiting RSPCA approval, but unlikely to get it. Absolutely free with every Dissuader comes the Parker *Cordon Mauve* cookery book, *150 Things You Can Do With A Swan.*

The Parker Psychological Bull Stiffener. A three-foot square Oxo Cube. One look at this and the bull dies of fright.

The Parker Fiddle-A-Diddle Double Standard Scales. Solid brass spring scales with an unobtrusive adjustment knob at the back. When you are weighing your own fish, a clockwise twist of the knob doubles the weight. When you are weighing your mate's fish, an anti-clockwise twist halves it. Leads to hours of jolly japes and missing teeth.

The Parker Stretchapoint Elastic Tape Measure. Unstretched, the inches are given in widths of half an inch each. So you measure your own fish with the tape measure held barely taut. See that seven-inch roach blossom immediately into a 14-inch monster!

To measure your mate's fish, stretch the measure as far as you can get away with. (Maximum stretch makes one inch span four normal inches.) Hear your mate's gasp of disbelief as you announce that his three-foot pike just scrapes in at nine inches. And then duck.

The Parker Bullshine Bifocal Camera. At last you can hold your fish out at arm's length, to make it look like something that Ernie Passmore has just dragged in, without your own dear handsome self looking like a sackful of out-of-focus porridge.

The bifocal lens, built on the principle of those funny-looking specs that people wear to make themselves look intelligent, gets you and the fish in pin-sharp detail. Only the fish looks three times as big as you do.

The Parker Send-A-Message-To-The-Mitherers T Shirt. A handsome T shirt is simulated schmatter with interchangeable tie-on panels bearing suitable messages. The panels are displayed on the back of the shirt to whichever onlooker is about to pester you next. Messages range from 'Nothing Doing', 'Not A Sausage', to 'Please Go Away' and 'Bugger Off'.

*   *   *

Don't Delay!! Order Today!!
No cheques or Sterling, please. Just send Deutschmarks, Guilders or fillet steaks.

They don't write 'em like this any more

Culture for the Masses time. With an examination of the limerick which, along with piranha tickling and gorilla wrestling, is one of the most neglected and underestimated art forms of our time.

My contribution to the rehabilitation of the limerick in polite society is this little collection of angling rhymes.

Consider the tragic fate of this poor lad:

> *There was a young angler from Leeds*
> *Who swallowed a packet of seeds.*
> > *His ganzi grew roots*
> > *Right down to his boots*
> *And his swingtip was covered in weeds.*

How often have we ourselves been in this next situation?

> *A specimen hunter from Wigan*
> *Cried, 'Hey up—I'm into a big 'un!'*
> > *He didn't half hoot*
> > *When out came a boot*
> *And a tree with a solitary twig on.*

When winter draws on, it can be fatal to leave winter drawers off. As this sad tale illustrates:

> *A goose-pimpled angler from Tottenham*
> *Cried, 'Oh dearie me—I've forgotten 'em!*
> > *'I've started to sneeze*
> > *'And without 'em I'll freeze.*
> *'What's warm I can put my cold bottom on?'*

My researches into the unpublished works of that great Jewish poet, Rabbi Burns, led to the discovery of this minor masterpiece:

> *A Scottish pike fisher from Troon*
> *Made a dreadful mistake with a spoon.*
> > *It gave quite a tilt*
> > *To the front of his kilt*
> *And his sporran just wouldn't lie doon.*

Angling is full of hazards. Even sitting out in the sun can result in the contraction of all sorts of nasties. As witness:

> *A ginger-haired angler from Eccles*
> *Broke out into terrible freckles.*
> *They spread from his tum*
> *Right round to his bum*
> *And up to the back of his neckles.*

Thank you. And goodnight.

The secret superbait

This is the true and unexpurgated story of the Parker Secret Superbait. Which hereafter is no longer secret, because I will give you the formula. Invented in a moment of desperation when Cousin Jim from Leeds turned up with his daft dog and we hadn't a maggot in the house.

Jim and Number One Son unearthed a dozen stringy worms from the bean patch, but I thought I'd better use something really special. Just to show my undoubted superiority as a wagger of the old wand. And here it comes:

Ingredients
1 small tin of Happy Pet, that revolting fish food that cats go potty over.
6 thick slices of bread and butter left over from last night's fish and chip supper.
A handful of sugar, snitched when the wife wasn't looking.
A handful of flour, with graded grains.

Method
Squidge everything together until it resembles a stiff kipper pudden or a pongy cannonball.

Down at the canal, Jim and Number One Son cast out and immediately reeled in a nice roach apiece.

I did not panic. With my Superbait, I could take my time. For the moment I could give all my attention, as a master should, to the meticulous details of tackling up. Confident that I should soon be pulling in fish like a berserking metronome.

I noticed with interest that the cannonball, as it lay ponging on the bank, was covered with wasps.

A good sign, I thought. If the wopsies like it, the fish won't be able to keep their little choppers off it, either.

All tackled up. Everything double checked. Let's get the show on the road. Bend down to pick up the Superbait. Which is not there.

It is in the mouth of a dog which is going hell for leather down the towpath.

An amazing burst of Parker speed from a standing start. The like of which had never been equalled since I found myself half a mile from the *White Hart* only five minutes this side of closing time.

Down in a flying tackle. Wellies akimbo. Catching the dog by the near hind leg. Grabbing the scruff of the neck with the free hand. Cummere, you—

'I say! That's my dog you've got there!'

'Sorry about that, missis. That's my flaming bait.'

Using the Parker wrestling skill and weight of tum to pin the beast to the ground. Prising the bait from its slavering jaws. Well, half of the bait. The other half went down with a 'gunk!' like a starving ostrich.

Another good sign, I thought. Wait till the little fishes get a sniff of this.

Back to the pitch. Where Jim and Number One Son are hauling in their third roach apiece. Watched by Jim's daft dog. Quiet, sensible, gentle dog, that. Not like the other raving tripehound.

The ragged piece of kipper pudden rounded again into a junior-size cannonball. Laid reverentially on the deck while I pick up my rod. Hook in hand, I turn back to the bait. Which again is not there. Not the tiniest crumb.

Only Jim's daft dog. Going, 'Burrrrp!'

This, I thought, is the last straw. The last goad. The final insult to the renowned Parker patience. The ultimate provocation. But it wasn't.

Jim's daft dog ran off yelping as a great hairy rat scuttled out of the hedge. The rat skidded to a stop at the place where the bait had lain, and sat bolt upright, chattering maniacally and sniffing the air in a quiver of frustration.

'You,' I roared, seeing the red mist before the eyes and swinging a power-packed wellie at the last of the freeloaders, '*You* can bugger off for a start!'

I felt sorry about that afterwards. The way you do.

... being extracts from the diaries and other documents of the Sludgethorpe Waltonians. This from the diary of Chukkitan Chansit, the club's Pakistani member.

The British Way

Trying to learn about the British way of life is now especially most confusing, as the British are no longer such, but Europeans.

Except for my very good friend Harry Turner, who is working on the next bench to me at Sludgethorpe Plastics.

Harry says he is booghered (a very old and traditional English word) if he is going to eat the frogs and wear the flaming jackboots. He is going to stay the Englishman.

And so I am asking him about the English way of life and whether he would be so very kind to tell me of its mysteries. How he chases the foxes and hunts the grouses and shoots at the peasants and phartridges. All in their due season, as I have read in *The Field* and *Country Life* sporting publications at the dentist's.

But Harry is saying the cobblers and that it would take a chocolate coloured twit like me to get the thing ah suppards. Ah suppards is yet another traditional English phrase which is meaning downside up.

Fishing, my friend Harry is saying, is the only way by which I will get to know about the English way of life.

So I am pleased, because I am knowing something of the fishing, and how the Englishmen are going out in the little fat ships called the trawlers and catching the cods of the Icelandic men. And how the Icelandic men are shooting the shells across the fronts of the little fat ships and how the English fishing men are throwing the nuts and bolts and the old cods at the Icelandic men.

Again Harry is saying the cobblers and that he is talking about the rod and line. Now I have it. Like the Queen Mum and the English lords, fishing for the noble salmon fish. With the help of a ghoolie, who is a Scottish gentleman.

Once more I am dropping the clangers and getting on the wick of Harry, who is saying that if I want to find out I must be joining the Sludgethorpe Waltonians, the world famous fishing association of which he is a very important member.

After two more days Harry is taking me to the meeting of the Sludgethorpe Waltonians and putting forward my name to the committee for membership. There is some opposition to my entry from Clogger Sedgewick and Tupper Brown, who also work at Sludgethorpe Plastics and who are disciples of the English lord Enoch Powell. They are constantly writing things on walls about nignogs out and bringing back the cats, which I am finding not at all to my liking.

My good friend Harry, however, is being very persuasive on my behalf and saying he will be giving the duffing over to anyone who is fancying his chances. So, in a very short time, I am declared the member.

Very good, I am saying to Harry, and when do we start catching the fishes? Harry is saying to me to hold the horses because I do not yet have the fishing rod, that it is dark outside, and that first we are having to wet the head of the baby.

I am very mystified because I do not have the baby or the horses, but Harry is telling me that it means I must be joining in with the bhoosing session and buying the first round.

The bhoosing is yet another old English custom and one which is very widespread. It means that a group of friends go into the place called the pub and the unlucky one buys drinks for all the others. This is known as the round. One by one, each in his turn buys the bhoose for all the others.

During the bhoosing session everybody is getting more and more jolly and telling strange stories of commercial travellers and farmers' daughters and being in general most friendly. There are some, however, who seem most reluctant to be buying the round, and Harry is telling such people to get the hand down, which is meaning to get the hand down in the pocket to reach the money for the bhoose.

We all had a most enjoyable evening, which is costing me much money, but is making me very happy. I am feeling very proud of my new chromium plated badge depicting the leaping fish and the most tasteful representation of the words *Sludgethorpe Waltonians*.

I think I am going to have some very jolly times.

Stopping the rot

Right, lads. Get fell in. We're closing our ranks to stop the rip-roaring inflation and get the old country back on its knees.

There is so much that anglers can do to ease the strain, both on our own pockets and the resources of the island as a whole.

What follows is the Parker Master Plan for Prosperity. Stick with it and we'll be out of the mire before you can say liquidity gap.

Little thin anglers can pair up and share a ganzi borrowed from a big fat one, taking an armhole each. Couple of snags. It only works well if one of them is left handed. And it can lead to ticklish situations when you're baiting up.

You can use only three wellies between two of you and tie your legs together as you do in a three-legged race. And no playing footsy.

Share the maggot. Pass it down the bank when you've used it for half an hour. When it gets to look a bit limp and empty, find somebody with a little mouth to give it the kiss of life and blow it up again. Difficult in most clubs. To find a member with a little mouth.

Stretch the worm. Two of you stand face to face, each taking a firm grip on one end of the worm, and start walking backwards. Stop before it goes off with an uncontrolled twang, or you might lose bits of it.

Using the mangle for worm stretching is not recommended. For every successful stretch you get three unsuccessful squashes.

Find other baits for free wherever you can. Shoo the sparrows off neighbours' bird tables and appropriate the bread crusts. Or creep up behind little old ladies feeding pigeons in the park and shout, 'Boo!'

Sort through restaurant dustbins for scraps of bacon fat, bits of sausage and shavings of luncheon meat. Get there early to avoid the rush by members of the Stock Exchange.

Use your bike instead of the car. And give other anglers a lift. With one on the handlebars, one on the crossbar and one on the rack at the back, four of you should be able to manage quite comfortably.

When the law flags you down and hints at a diet of bread and water for the rest of your natural, appeal to the world renowned sense of humour of the British bobby. Then hold out your wrists for the cuffs.

Fish only during the hours of daylight. Night fishers who find the adjustment difficult can try closing their eyes or pulling their bobbly hats down over their noses.

Instead of buying rounds in the pub of four pints at a time, ask for one pint and four straws. To avoid friction, insist that everybody sucks at the same rate. Anyone caught cheating to have his straw knotted. Anyone caught cheating twice to have his neck knotted.

* * *

Makes you wonder whether it's as bad as all that, though, when you read of some of the rents being asked for salmon stretches.

An article in one of the quality Sundays reported the offer of the yearly rights for a 1¾-mile stretch on the River Wye, with the chance of 150 salmon in the season. The stretch was expected to fetch more than £200,000.

This would work out at £1,300 a fish, give or take the loose change. And with some stretches the estate agents were expecting more than £2,000 a fish.

'It makyth me to spit, Horatio,' as the Immortal Bard once said, over a pint at *The Mermaid.*

But don't laugh. At these prices, the English noble lords who used to frequent rivers like the Wye for a quick aristocratic flick will be elbowed out. The only ones with the ready cash to move in will be the oil sheikhs and the upright American politicians who haven't got round to paying any taxes for the past twenty years.

And where will the nobility finish up? With us, brothers. Along the cut. And it will cost us.

A few coronets bobbing about the canal are bound to raise the tone. But a mass migration of belted earls and duffed-up dukes to the coarse-fishing scene will raise rents and prices for bait and tackle as well.

Let's face it, they're high enough already.

'Half a dozen worms, sir? Certainly. That will be a pound.'

'Here's thirty bob. I trod on a maggot on my way in.'

And the overcrowding. If the chinless ones are going to turn up at the canal with a gillie, a maggot putter-onner, a valet to brush the cowflop off the noble wellies and a butler to serve the cheese butties and light ale, where are *we* going to sit?

How can we expect to get served in the pubs when the landords are fawning round the ermine and telling the rest of us to get back in the Public or wait in the yard?

Will we ever hear again of superstars like Ivan Marks, Kevin Ashurst or Cliff Parker? When the picture space in *Angling Times* is taken up by full frontals of debs' delights holding up ninety quid bleak or £500 fungus-ridden roach?

When the news pages are full of stories which begin:

The Hon Augustus 'Mad Dan' Thwartfarthing paid a record £84,000 this week for a year's fishing rights on a 350-yard stretch of the Natswiddle and Rubbidge Canal . . .

When the Gossip Column is filled with headlines like:

'NO' TO ROYAL ROMANCE, SAYS SLUDGETHORPE MATCH ACE

Still, it's an ill wind which blows nobody a bob or two. Some of the more impoverished angling clubs might find the influx of aristocratic capital a real shot in the arm for the darts fund and Christmas club.

And the entrepreneurs, the quick-witted lads like myself, might be able to cash in.

That's why I'm not fishing much at the moment. I'm busy enlarging the frog pond at the back.

Step right this way, Your Noble Sirship. Have I got the gudgeon for you . . .

Don't let the wife read this

The first month of the season is the time when sport-starved anglers rush down to the water in fevers of frustrated enthusiasm. And spend every spare waking minute wagging the old rod.

It is also the time when they suffer repeated and vicious physical assaults from wives who have become too used to having them around.

If you don't believe me, look into the Casualty Ward at Manchester Royal Infirmary on Monday mornings. Blokes with saucepans jammed over their ears, with their meal still inside; blokes with keepnets wrenched over their heads right down to their feet, leaving them room only for a geisha girl shuffle to the operating theatre; blokes with lacerations and contusions from rolling-pins, fire tongs, pokers, frying-pans, bread knives, meat cleavers, grandfather clocks and pussycats.

Indeed, the female of the species is more deadly than the male, as my old mate Kipling used to say.

(He was not an easy man to get on with, old Kippers. In fact he was ruddy 'ard. Get it? All right. All right. It may be old, but at least it's clean.)

What we need, until the little women have got used to the season again, is a completely new set of excuses for getting back home late and in dog order. Not only new excuses, but ones which:

a) Are valid in the context of our troubled and rapidly changing society.

b) Show you in a noble, heroic or self-sacrificing light.

c) Bring out her latent compassion. (It's in there somewhere, lads.)

Let's try some socially valid ones first:

'I was walking along this badly-lit short cut when I was jumped on by four desperate muggers who beat me up and robbed me of all my money. I was left for dead until my stalwart comrades stumbled across my prostrate form and carried me into the *Queen and Cobbler* for urgently needed attention.'

*　　　*　　　*

'I was on this boat which was boarded by the Irish Navy. We had to heave-to for three hours while they combed the craft from stem to stern in search of an illegal consignment of shillelaghs.'

*　　　*　　　*

'I was just stepping from the rowing boat on to the beach in pitch darkness when some nasty policemen jumped on me and took me for questioning as an illegal immigrant. It was four hours before they would release me, on account of the healthy tan I had acquired during the day.'

*　　*　　*

Then there was your involvement in a civil disorder:

'There was this riot on the bank after the match, my dear, in which I was unavoidably involved. It took me a long time to fight my way out of the fracas and rush to the shelter of our dear little home.'

Not mentioning that you started the punch-up in the first place by accusing the opposing team of rigging the scales at the weigh-in.

Now some in a noble or self-sacrificing vein. First, in search of knowledge:

'I was passing this taxidermist's when I notice them stuffing an opah. An opah, as you doubtless know, my dear, is a very large fish. Which takes an awful lot of stuffing. The hours I spent in observation were not wasted. Should I ever be so fortunate as to catch an opah, I know now exactly how and where to stuff it.'

Helping to conserve the defenceless creatures threatened by our increasingly hostile environment:

'I was hurrying to your side, my dear, when I stopped to help a toad across the road/stopped to guide a frog in the fog.'

On an errand of mercy:

'I was delayed, my pet, because I stopped to save an unfortunate fellow angler from drowning.'

You omit to tell her that he was drowning in draught bitter and that you saved him from becoming waterlogged by helping him to drink it.

And yet another errand of mercy:

'I saw a young angler in distress. And stayed to give the kiss of life.'

Not mentioning that the young angler was 23-year-old Maisie Fruit. And that dis dress you saw her in was a very short polka-dot job with a cleavage down to her appendix scar.

Here's one in which heroism and the appeal to compassion combine:

'I was the winner of the match, my love. The hero of the hour. So pleased were my comrades, such was their joy and delight, that I could do no other than accompany them to the *Cock and Bottle* for a celebratory drink. I regret to inform you that my hard-earned winnings are no more, it being the custom of our club for the winner to pay for the celebration.'

37

For bringing out the real compassion, there's nothing like an injury:

'I was delayed, Moon of my Delight, because of this nasty wound I received from a carelessly placed rod rest. It took my dear comrades quite a while to find somebody equipped and qualified to dispense and administer the necessary medication.'

Which, roughly translated, means that you backed into the rod rest you'd left leaning against the basket, sharp side up, and that you slowed your mates down in their search for a pub which stocked aspirins, Elastoplast and John Jamieson's.

There you are, lads. That little lot should see you through the first month all right. If it doesn't I'll see you in the Infirmary.

Disguise and datguise

We're always being told that half the battle is getting to the water undetected by the fish. And staying that way.

There are dangers in camouflage, however, of which every angler should be aware. If the disguise is too good, you could be in real danger of losing valuable and interesting bits of yourself, not to say in peril of your young and happy life.

Before I discuss the dangers, I should like to introduce you to two new disguises guaranteed to be absolutely safe in most normal fishing conditions:

1. The Parker Plastic Simulated Henhouse. Nobody suspects a henhouse. Nor do people do nasty things to it, like chop it down. Wear this henhouse to the bank and watch your catches soar. Just send chest and inside leg measurements to receive:

> *Henhouse, complete with foxproof flies*
> *Long playing record of a pregnant hen*
> *Set of six pot eggs*
> *Bag of self-adhesive feathers*

Only £350·02½ plus VAT.

2. The Parker Simulated Parker Kit. With this kit you can disguise yourself to look like Cliff Parker. The fish immediately think they are perfectly safe. Kit comprises:

> *Flashing teeth*
> *Steely blue eyes*
> *Flowing hair*
> *Noble brow*
> *Rippling muscles*

All in high grade simulated plastic. Only £550·17½ plus VAT. No cheques, please, but will accept empties.

* * *

The trouble with the traditional disguises is that they bring with them a whole host of problems. Take decking yourself out with leafy twigs and grass. An innocent and safe enough pastime, you may think.

But those twigs and blades of grass are riddled with such diseases as black spot, brown rot, rust and dingle wilt. You could come back

from a day's fishing all spotted, rotted, rusted, and with your dingle well and truly wilted.

You could get attacked by creatures. The twigs are full of voracious insects like sawflies, earwigs, and capsid bugs. It's no fun coming back with your flies sawn, your ears wiggered and your capsids buggered.

As you sit there, indistinguishable from the surrounding vegetation, you can get sprayed with all sorts of insecticide. You run the risk of being fertilised as well. Not so bad when it's chemical fertiliser. But when you've got a farmer who believes there's nowt like old-fashioned muck, you could cop for something really revolting.

Even dressing up as a full-size tree does not remove all the problems. You are still exposed to the ravages of woodworm and Dutch elm disease. The first symptom of woodworm is a nose full of holes. You can tell when you've got Dutch elm disease by the way bits keep falling off you.

Dogs come along and get all anti-social. It's no use hissing at them to clear off, because they hiss back. All over your kneecaps.

Courting couples carve all over you. Hearts, arrows, and stupid messages like, 'Wayne loves Marlene. True.' Half the time Wayne can't spell Marlene and needs half a dozen goes to get it right.

Forestry work presents the biggest danger. If somebody comes along and chalks a big white cross on your bum, move out fast. Otherwise they'll be calling you Shorty.

During the summer there are lots of pantomime horse and cow

costumes for hire at special cheap rates. Anglers often club together for a costume and go fishing in pairs.

If you go in for this, make sure you get the front legs. The bloke at the back has a lot to put up with.

Keep in mind, as an awful warning, the story of the two anglers who were making their way to the water, dressed as a cow, when a bull was let into the field.

'Hey,' said the one at the back. 'There's a bull coming after us at a hell of a lick. What shall we do?'

'I'm going to bend down and eat this grass,' said the one at the front. '*You* better brace yourself.'

Jolly japes for buddy mates

One story which crops up every year is about the lad on the sea fishing trip who goes puky-groo over the side of the boat and loses his false teeth. And his mate ties his own false teeth to his line and pretends to catch them. And the first feller finds they won't fit and throws them back into the sea.

Laugh? I could kiss the cat. Serves the second feller right for doing naughties on his mate. Har har. Ho ho. Tee hee. Hyuk hyuk.

I'm all in favour of encouraging the trend. Getting stuck in while it's still warm. Getting some laughs back into the game. With hilarious pranks like those listed hereafter. For the consequences of which I take no responsibility whatsoever. Me being a coward, like.

Cut the end off his landing net. Gasp as the ten-pound barbel slides over the top. Titter as it shoots straight through the bottom and smashes the line.

Undercut the bank. Doesn't take long with an army surplus entrenching tool. With which those of us who answered our country's etc. are familiar. Note the surprised expression on your mate's face as the whole shoot collapses beneath him and he falls into the water. Chortle as he goes under for the third time.

Saw through the legs of his basket. Fall about as it collapses and he gets a bumful of splinters.

Put a rat trap in his bait tin. Guffaw as the steel spring snaps over his casting hand. Shout jolly greetings like, 'Hi there, Lefty!'

Grate soap into his groundbait. Marvel as his swim bubbles. Be amazed as the fish come spluttering to the top. Offer stupid words of comfort. Like, 'Cleanliness is next to godliness is what I always say. Har har.'

Inject his lobs with gelignite. Rock with laughter as he sticks in the hook and goes off bang.

Tell the bailiff that your mate's membership card is a forgery. A very skilful forgery, which only a super-intelligent bailiff such as himself could detect. Thrill as the argument gets heated. Cheer as the bailiff puts on the approved Police College armlock and hairgrip and escorts your mate back to the bailiffs' social club to help in enquiries.

He who plays practical jokes must be prepared to take them. When you find yourself sinking slowly in the cut, your nostrils stuffed with pinkies, a live pike up each trouser leg and your wellies filled with quick drying cement, just remember that it's all good, clean fun.

And that it's nowt to do with me.

... being extracts from the diaries and other documents of the Sludgethorpe Waltonians. This from the diary of Chukkitan Chansit, the newly enrolled Pakistani member.

How I am striking the fish

It was most sad that, a few weeks after I am joining the excellent Waltonians, the time is coming for the fishes to be breeding.

Here I agree with my good friend Harry Turner, who says that three months to be doing sexy things is far too long. Especially for fishes, whose imagination is limited.

However, I am using the remaining time well, thanks being to Harry who is taking me several times to the canal to learn the skills of rod and line.

Firstly he is telling me that coarse fishing is a very fine and delicate way of taking the fish. I am asking him why then is it called coarse. He is telling me to stop asking the daft questions, and leaving me very puzzled.

Then he is showing me how to be fixing the float and the shots and the hook. And how to be putting on the maggot at the end where the eyes are.

He is telling me that the eyes are not eyes because they are at the wrong end. When I am asking what they are, he is telling me again to stop asking the daft questions. Doubtless there are some things which are very secret and which cannot be revealed until the pupil is very experienced in angling ways.

I am finding it most difficult at first to do the casting into the water. Several times I am hooking trees and once I am hooking Harry. He was most noble and brave about it, although he was using some words which were quite unfamiliar to me.

Eventually I am casting out far enough into the water to give Harry much pleasure, and the top of the float is sticking up. Suddenly it is sticking down and going away under the water.

Harry is shouting at me to strike, and I am telling him that we are not working and therefore cannot be striking. Then I am feeling something pulling on the line and I am winding in the handle of the reel according to Harry's instructions. He is being very excited and shouting most loudly, 'Don't panic!'

To my very great amazement, there is a little fish sticking on the hook. While Harry is taking out the hook I am asking him how do we cook the fish and can it be curried and served with peppers.

Harry is telling me that we are not to be eating the fish and that first it must be put in the keeping net, and then put back into the water.

This I am finding very strange and am asking why we are taking all the trouble when we are not to be eating the fish. And if we are to be putting it back, why first must it be spending time in the keeping net.

Harry is saying, 'Just because, that's why'. Again I am realising that this is another of the mysteries of the fishing which will be revealed to me in time.

Towards eleven o'clock in the morning, Harry is getting a little impatient with my questioning. I am thinking that perhaps I should not be prying too deeply and getting up the nose of my very good friend.

At eleven o'clock Harry is saying that the fish will be biting no more for some time. I am admiring Harry's knowledge of the fishes' habits and asking him how he is knowing this valuable piece of information.

Harry is saying that eleven o'clock is time for the opening of the bhooser, and that all the fish in the canal have been trained to stop eating so as not to be interfering with the social habits of the fishermen.

I am marvelling at the English power over animals when I realise that Harry is pulling my legs and taking the mickey from me, and that he wants to go to the pub for the bhoosing.

We are having some very pleasant bhoosing in *The Bricklayer's Arms*, in spite of the large landlord who was not seeming very pleased to see us, and then we are going back to the canal.

We are not doing much more fishing because I am still unused to the effects of the bhoosing and am being most unfortunate in falling in the water.

On the way home Harry is telling me that I am to be catching the fish with the rod and not to be diving in after them, and we are having jolly laughings over this.

Next morning I am sneezing most heartily.

Crocks' corner

Angling has a higher incidence of accidents and ailments than any other sport or pastime, excepting only Russian roulette and high wire tap dancing.

Unfortunately—even tragically—many hard-pressed general practitioners fail to recognise the symptoms of angling ills and injuries and treat them as if they were sustained in the normal course of normal events by normal people.

The reason so few of these injuries and ailments are known to medicine at large is because:

a) They manifest themselves in locations far from the teaching hospitals, the emergency services, the media, policemen, sociologists, penal reformers or any kind of mass human activity.

b) They are often mistaken for other injuries or ailments, such as being run over by a tram, bitten by a ravening Tasmanian Devil, exposed on the northern slopes of Kanchenjunga for a week, or crushed in the arms of a hash-crazed grizzly.

In an effort to rectify the situation and to give GPs the guidance they will never find in *The Lancet* in a million years, should they live so long, the Parker Institute for the Study of Anglers' Nasties is making available the results of years of detailed observation and painful personal experience.

To begin at the beginning. Recognition. How will the doctor know that the stranger who confronts him is, indeed, an angler?

Should he come in on any day but Monday, he will look quite normal, be dressed in normal clothes, and will have the usual skiver's shuffle as he walks sideways into the consulting room.

He will announce that his back is due to play him up on Wednesday afternoon, or that his hammer toes are bound to lock rigid on Friday, and could he please have a note for work?

Subtle and sympathetic questioning will elicit the information that his impending back trouble is due to the fact that the idiot club secretary put him down for a midweek match, or that his mate works in a shop and gets Wednesday afternoon off for early closing day.

The seizure of his hammer toes on Friday is being brought on by the fact that he wants to spend the day not only fishing, but ground-baiting a few secret swims so that he can be straight in there with a chance first thing Saturday morning.

What do you do, as a general practitioner bound by the Hippocratic Oath? You give him a note, that's what you do. Malingerer he may be, but his malingering stems from a deep-rooted psychological maladjustment brought about by the pressures of the artificial and materialistic society we find ourselves in. Or from bone idleness.

What, I ask you, is the good of putting men on the moon when a bloke can't even have a weekday of peace and quiet by the river, redressing the spiritual imbalance of an urbanised life pattern? I mean, nobody at the factory consulted *him* about laying on shifts for Wednesday and Friday, did they?

Now, the angler who stumbles into morning surgery on *Monday* has *been* fishing. All weekend since Friday evening. And has not had a wink of sleep. His stumbling walk and gasping for breath are not assumed; they're for real.

He can be identified, firstly, by his clothes. Few people on a Monday morning walk around dressed in (a) wellies, bobbly hat, ankle-length raincoat tied with string and army surplus mittens, or (b) camouflage jacket/paratrooper's smock, Castro-type hat, waterproof trousers and ammunition boots.

Identification can be confirmed by a few simple observations. Look at the eyes. Bloodshot, bleary, watering, unfocused, sometimes crossed, set in a doughy face which carries three days' growth of stubble.

Say, 'Good morning'. A true weekend angler will reply only, 'Wha . . . ? Wha . . . wha . . . ?' while looking blankly around the room as if trying to remember where he is.

Look at the hands. They will be a quarter-inch thick in the most revolting mixture of fish and worm slime, scales, old maggot skins, breadpaste and crumbs of cheese.

Smell his breath. It will be a compound of cheese and pickle butties, draught bitter, rum and scotch, stale as all getout and perfectly unbearable. Remember not to strike a match while he is breathing out.

Ask him to strip off. If you have the time, that is, and can stand what is to come. By the time he has removed his outer coat, and then shed three pullovers, two shirts, a string vest, a red flannel comforter, two pairs of trousers, a pair of long johns, a pair of Thermogene Y-fronts, one pair of wellingtons, a pair of seaboot stockings, two pairs of socks and a couple of hot water bottles, you will realise that you are dealing with no ordinary man.

Ask him to bend over. Now take a look. (It's not a pretty sight, but force yourself.) If he bears the telltale wicker weave pattern of a fishing basket across both buttocks, he is suffering from the first stages of the dreaded Basket Bum, and can therefore be identified beyond any reasonable doubt as an angler.

As he peels off, keep your eyes open for other clues. From the

Anyone for thrutching?

I have this mate called Long Tall Tony who climbs mountains and is always going on about thrutching.

'Sssh!' I said once in a posh pub. (You could tell it was posh by the way the barmaid stuck out her little finger when she picked her nose.) 'Sssh! There are ladies present.'

'No,' he said. 'Thrutching means having a hard climb. Really having to work to get to the top. I bet you have to do lots of thrutching when you're out fishing.'

'No,' I said. 'We don't go in for things like that.'

I lied. We do. Thrutching really means doing things the hard way. Which, in angling terms, is fishing by the book. Doing what the experts tell you. Which always works out more expensive, more nerve-racking and more muscle-bending than doing what comes naturally.

Thrutching means breeding your own maggots. Having the shed, the garage, the loft or the back end of the yard permanently ponging like a knacker's yard in a bank holiday heatwave. And neighbours getting up petitions.

Thrutching means tying your own flies. Going boss-eyed and getting the trembles of the fingertips which precede the total seizing up known as Dapper's Doom. All to produce something that looks like a badly made bog brush.

Thrutching means stewing your own hemp. And having the wife storm out of the house. With the kids. And the pussycat and hamster. Pausing only to call in at the solicitor's to file papers for mental cruelty and misuse of her nonstick pans.

Thrutching means getting your own wasp grubs. At short notice. And thereby having neither the protection nor the armoury. Going out on a Sunday afternoon to Big McGinty's compost heap. Armed only with a spade, a bait tin and an aerosol thing that claims to kill all flying nasties stone dead. Leaving you backing away, squirting like mad at the kamikaze wopsies who don't know they're supposed to be dead, and who sting you in places you never knew you had.

Thrutching means making your own groundbait. To the jealously guarded secret formula. Setting fire to the oven in which you left the breadcrusts while you popped out to the *Nag and Knocker*. Forgetting that 475 degrees Fahrenheit or Gas No. 9 is not exactly a low light. Coming back to be greeted by the jolly lads from the fire brigade. Who haven't been round since you tried to bake the wasp grubs.

Thrutching means making your own floats. Slicing chunks off the left thumb as you shave down bits of balsa or trim the old quills. To produce a thing like a pot-bellied ballpoint refill that sinks at the first cast. At a cost of only £15·37 plus VAT and french polishing the table.

Thrutching means collecting natural bait from the hedgerows. Like elderberries. Which come off the trees in lovely great bunches and fill up the spare room until you can get round to preserving them. Leaving plenty of time for the forty thousand earwigs hidden in the bunches to abscond and take over the whole house. Playing hell with the cat's peace of mind.

Thrutching means stalking the fish. Crawling to the water in camouflage gear and with burnt cork or Cherry Blossom all over the old mush. Which gives you spots and gets you arrested as an IRA suspect or illegal immigrant. And which, if you don't actually overshoot the bank and fall in, leaves you with earwigs in your ears, hares in your hair, daddies in your longlegs and bot flies up your nose.

The lesson is plain. If you feel a thrutch coming on, go and sit in a nice safe pub until it wears off.

Alternatively, be strong. Nip it in the bud. Knock it on the head. Kick it in the thrutch.

Eata buncha frogsa day

Poddy the Poacher appeared in court wearing a frogman's suit with flippers and with pheasant feathers in his hair. As one does.

Accused of cruelty by frog swallowing. Just another everyday, run-of-the-mill case for Market Drayton magistrates.

(Ho hum, another frog swallower. That's the fourteenth today. What a drag. Repeat after me . . . 'I solemnly swear . . . ')

Poddy got off. Free to wander round the pubs scoffing live frogs to his heart's content. Preparing for his attempt on the current frog-swallowing record of five in 65 seconds. Held by this Irishman called McNamara.

His revolting pastime was cleared after his solicitor had pointed out that swallowing live frogs was no worse than using them as pike bait.

Indeed, it's probably a sight more pleasant for the poor old frog. Straight down in a wash of wallop instead of hanging about for hours underwater with a hook up your bum.

(Mind you, I would prefer to be swallowed by someone other than Poddy. I don't fancy him at all, wet suit or no wet suit. Brigitte Bardot or Sophia Loren would be much more like. I could die happy then.)

Where was I? Yes, it doesn't say much for the livebaiters, does it? When, on the strength of what they're doing every weekend, little fellers in frogmen's suits with feathers in their hair can flip-flop into a pub and knock back a couple of live frogs with their black and tans.

The livebaiting hassle could go on forever. But I would suggest some records which Poddy might be better aiming for, and which the livebaiters might like to attempt as well:

The Number of Alligators Sharing the Bath Record. Present record 12, held by Fred 'Shorthouse' Loonibinn.

The Live Piranha Swallowing Record. Present record 33, held by Don Jose Juan Carlos El Toro Miguel Chuckerbutty, recipient of the world's first stomach transplant.

The Sharing a Sack With Congers Record. This is a time record. The challenger is put in a sack full of live congers and the top is tied tight. He is released as soon as he screams. Present holder John 'Two-Fingered Jack' Gormless, with a time of 1·3 seconds.

The Pike Down the Trousers Record. Live pike are stuffed down the challenger's trousers, which are tied at the knees. Every five seconds they are given a whack with a landing net handle to liven them up. The present record is 17, held by Patricia (formerly Paddy) MacHooligan.

A lot of them about

It was an interesting news story about the two American anglers being taken into a flying saucer by creatures with crablike hands.

I believe it, every word, because one night Big McGinty and I saw two flying saucers circling each other.

McGinty pulled out his night driving glasses to get a better look, but he dropped them and I stood on them in the dark. A pity, that.

Next day I mentioned the saucers to Ben, landlord of the *White Hart*.

'What time was it?' asked Ben, looking at me sideways.

'About eleven o'clock.'

'Oh, arr,' said Ben. 'There's a lot of 'em about at that time o' night . . . '

I think anglers see more of the paranormal, supernatural and just the plain unusual, than the average bloke. Not only is the angler more intelligent, sensitive and receptive, but he is also about at odd hours and doing odd things. The trouble is that nobody believes the stories afterwards.

Like the parrot. One morning, very early, I was taking Mad Mac fishing in my car. On the outskirts of Hemel Hempstead I swerved suddenly, waking Mac up.

'Bloody parrots!' I said. 'Walking into the road like that without looking . . . '

Mac looked at me very strangely for the rest of the day. But a parrot *had* stepped off the kerb straight in front of the car. I wished, in a way, that I hadn't missed it. At least then I could have shown Mac a flat parrot as proof.

Later that day we were thawing out in a pub and Mac was gazing absently out of the window. Suddenly he said, 'Hey—I take it all back, buddy mate. There's a parrot in that tree.'

And so there was. But it wasn't the same parrot. Mine was sort of brown and white, and this was a highly coloured job.

'Excuse me,' I said to the landlord. 'Do you have much trouble with parrots around here?'

'No . . . it's purple cockatoos we get in here mate. Generally round about half past ten. Crawling all over the walls, they are. You sure you're all right?'

I pointed through the window, but all that was on the tree was leaves. The parrot had disappeared. So Mac and I left.

'Bloody parrots,' I said.

'Bloody parrots,' said Mac.

And a voice from the tree said, 'Oo's a cheeky boy, then?'

Why I am no longer God

In the days when we used English money and a pound note was worth passing across a pub counter, Number One Son was knee high to the cat and he worshipped his dad.

Many's the time I've glowed with pride, eavesdropping on his chats with his mates, to hear him say, 'My dad can catch more fish than your dad. My dad's stronger than your dad. My dad's braver than your dad. He was in the desert and he killed lots and lots of Romans.'

Later, as his horizons widened and he knew me better, it could be disconcerting to overhear his more sophisticated values. 'My dad's hairier than your dad. My dad can burp louder than your dad. My dad can sup more pints than your dad.'

Bless him. His heart was in the right place.

But dear me, I thought. This lad of mine must not grow up thinking that I am God. One of these days I must disabuse him. He must find out, gradually, that under this superhuman exterior dwells an ordinary, fallible human being.

I needn't have worried. He's found out for himself. It's his age that's done it. And last season's fishing.

It started on the River Ouzel, near Leighton Buzzard. Where I pointed out to him all the places likely to hold fish. And in which places we fished. Where for weeks neither of us got a nibble. Until one day he wandered off on his own further downriver, naked into the world and without benefit of parental counsel, to try for himself. And came back with a netful of perch, roach and chub.

'You old twit,' he said.

Another time, on that same river, we passed a lie under some willows.

'Not there, son of mine,' I said. 'Hie with me to yonder deeps on the bends and there we shall catch perch of size and numbers beyond your wildest imaginings.'

Three hours later there had been nary a tremble.

'I'm going back to that lie further down,' he said.

'No use, lad. See how this bank has filled up with people, how every swim has been taken. There's bound to be somebody in that lie by this time. Not that it will do him any good.'

Another eventless hour passed, and we packed up. When we got to the lie under the willows, it was empty.

'You said . . . ' began Number One Son.

'I know what I said, and for once it appears I was wrong. But you'd have caught nowt there anyway.'

The timing was uncanny. As the last word fell from my lips, a monstrous fish—either chub or pike—leapt out of the lie and fell back on its side with a splash that left the willows dripping.

'You old twit,' said Number One Son.

On holiday near Great Yarmouth, I thought I'd regain some respect. Number One Son's athletic activities had displaced a bone in his coccyx. (Yes, you do have a bone there. Look it up.) This meant that offshore boat fishing was out for the time being, and he would have to rely on his old man's skill and experience to find the fish under gentler conditions.

He wanted to fish Fritton Lake, and produced a leaflet extolling its fish and facilities.

'Pish,' I said. 'And tush. Sheer commercialism. It'll be over-crowded, overfished, full of boaters and squawking kids. Come with papa to the unspoilt, little-known stretch of water I have just discovered on this map.'

Suspiciously quiet it was, when we got there. It dawned upon me as the day wore on, ever and ever fishless, that the reason the water was unspoilt was that it had nothing worth spoiling; the reason it was so little known was that nobody wanted to know it.

'You old twit,' said Number One Son.

Next day I took him out on a plastic rowboat on a little broad.

It was a very eventful trip. I ran the boat aground twice, and went over the side with the anchor when I dropped it (well, how was I to know it was that heavy?). And when we were finally anchored and I'd climbed back in, the boat kept swinging round in large circles, taking us yards away from the spot we'd groundbaited and leaving us most of the time facing the wrong way. Oh, yes, we had some jolly adventures. But no fish.

'You old twit,' said Number One Son.

Next day we went on the pier at Great Yarmouth. We had to use handlines because I'd left the rods behind.

Down on the jetty I summed up the situation.

'The tide's coming in nicely, son. And I reckon we'd be best fishing on the right-hand side.'

An hour later, Number One Son pointed out that there was less water under the pier than there had been, on account of the tide going out rapidly, and that everybody else was fishing on the left-hand side.

'Look,' I said, 'I can't be right all the time, can I? And anybody can just follow the crowd. Give me your handline, Sunshine, and I will show you a cast which will take the bait far beyond those of the sheeplike amateurs on the other side. This cast will amaze you.'

It did. And me, too, because I had my foot on the line. I stood there like Rameses II, wrapped in line from head to foot and stunned from the impact of the 2 oz lead behind my earhole.

Number One Son carefully unwrapped me.

'I think,' he said, as he removed the ripe squid tentacle from my left nostril, 'that we'd better call it a day.'

*   *   *

The final disillusionment came, back home, with the dropping through the letter-box of *Angling Times*. Number One Son grabbed it first and dived back into bed.

The first page he opened carried a feature on Fritton Lake. '175 ACRES OF PARADISE FOR ANGLERS' said the headline. And the text was dripping with drool-making reports of catches—a pike of 35 lb, eels netted up to 9½ lb and what seemed to be common-place bags of bream topping 150 lb.

From the bedroom came an agonised scream.

'YOU OLD TWIT!'

'All right. All *right*,' I said. 'So nobody's perfect ... '

The Sludgethorpe Diaries

... being extracts from the diaries and other documents of the Sludgethorpe Waltonians. This being the text of the speech delivered by Mr Wilfred Harbottle, Hon Chairman of the Waltonians, on the occasion of the club's end-of-season social and prizegiving.

A very good year

Ladies and Gentlemen,

It gives me great pleasure to welcome you all here this evening.

I do not propose to keep you long from the real business of the prizegiving and jollifications, but would like to say a few words about the triumphs and tragedies of the season past.

It grieves me to use the word 'tragedy', but use it I must. As you all know, late last year, our beloved Albert Rowbottom departed this life. Shuffled off, as it were, this mortal coil.

One of our veteran members, a great stalwart of the social nights, treasurer of the Christmas Club and chairman of the Indoor Games Committee, Albert had the misfortune to take the wrong turning in the fog after an Old Comrades' Reunion at the British Legion.

He fell into the canal at the Foundry Road lock, after apparently mistaking the lock gates for the bridge. His cries were heard by some of his fellow Legionaires and he was pulled out, apparently none the worse for wear. Indeed, his friends told me that all the way home he was regaling them with choruses of *Comrades*, *Goodbye Dolly Gray*, and *The White Cliffs of Dover*.

But, sadly, he caught a chill from which he never recovered.

The Christmas Club and bar accounts were taken over by Mr Dipper Purvis, who shortly afterwards suddenly and mysteriously left the district. The valiant and untiring efforts of the Sludgethorpe Constabulary eventually traced him to the Isle of Man. The Christmas Club funds and a week's bar takings, which disappeared at the same time as Mr Purvis, were never recovered. The case comes up next month.

To happier tidings. Our annual Derby match against Slagville Piscatorials was won narrowly but decisively, thanks mainly to the extraordinary individual catch recorded by Mr Chalky White.

The objections lodged at the weigh-in by the Piscatorials were discounted by the neutral Chief Steward, Mr Arthur Micklethwaite. As Mr Micklethwaite so rightly pointed out, the apparently soapy appearance of the stretch fished by the Piscatorials' champion matchman could have been caused only by an accidental discharge from a passing boat.

The herring weighed in with Mr White's catch, Mr Micklethwaite averred, was still further evidence of the growing tendency of sea fish to swim inland during inclement weather. The herring was, regrettably, dead, obviously exhausted by its long journey from the sea, the effects of canal water on its metabolism, and the spirited fight it put up on Mr White's line.

Mr Micklethwaite is here tonight to join us in our festivities. I was surprised and delighted, earlier in the evening, to discover that he is related by marriage to our redoubtable Mr White.

Hearty congratulations are due to Mrs Lulu Waghorn, the young and lovely lady wife of the former secretary of our Veterans' Committee. Last week Mrs Waghorn gave birth to a bouncing baby boy. This has no doubt done a great deal to cheer up Mr Waghorn, who, as you know, has been in hospital for the past twelve months with severe back trouble.

Among the prizes which will later be distributed are several donated by kind business and social contacts of our little club. Mr Edward Fanshawe, mine host of *The Bricklayer's Arms*—known affectionately to us all as Big Eddie—has donated a set of darts to be used exclusively by our club members on their visits to his delightful hostelry.

He accompanies them with a humorous little note, saying that they will stop us bending the points on the arrows belonging to his own darts club, that he has had the wall behind the board re-plastered, and that Mr Cyril Higginson—whose nose, you will remember, was unfortunately pierced by a stray arrow thrown by our late Mr Rowbottom—is now almost fully recovered and only has trouble when he blows his nose.

Another unexpected addition to our store of gifts is a box of scented soaps from our old rivals, Slagville Piscatorials.

With it comes the wish that, on the occasion of our next Derby match, the best team may win. They even offer their condolences in advance. What a sporting lot they are, ladies and gentlemen.

On that note of piscatorial fraternity I will end my little dissertation. Adding only the heartfelt wish that next season will be as joyful and rewarding as the last.

. . . and keep the change

Up and up go the prices of bait and tackle. Perhaps we've been too lucky for too long, but it does come hard when the cost of the working man's simple and innocent pastime starts to verge on the prohibitive.

I mean, it's not as if we were gambling, or boozing, or running around with women, is it?

Is it?

Pausing not for an answer, and looking neither to the left nor the right, he moves on to the next bit. Which is the Patented Parker System of Piscatorial Barter.

The more I think about this idea, the crummier it seems, but that's probably what all the Great Minds of History thought when the still, small voice went *Boi-oi-oing*!

This system would do away with money and return to the old barter system. We'd just carry fishing baits and gear around to swop. A table of relative currency values would probably go something like:

2 pinkies	=	1 special
2 specials	=	1 gozzer
2 gozzers	=	1 wasp grub
2 wasp grubs	=	1 lob
3 lobs	=	1 hook
4 hooks	=	1 float
2 floats	=	1 swingtip
2 swingtips	=	1 bobbly hat
5 bobbly hats	=	1 wellie

. . . and so on.

The advantages of the system are obvious even to the dimmest. (Get out of that. You can't, can you?) Having, by common consent, agreed to them, let us look at some of the drawbacks.

Things could get awkward at times, having to carry around pocketsful of wellies, bobbly hats, pinkies and specials. You could have a back pocket full of small change one minute and, should somebody inadvertently bump into you, a horrible squashy mess the next.

It might be difficult to find a landlord who would accept a handful of specials and lobs in return for a couple of pints of bitter. And if you were to say, 'One for yourself, landlord,' what would you offer him for the round? Eight six-inch lobs and a couple of inches snipped off a ninth? Or would you give him all nine and say, 'Keep the change'?

Flag-day collectors might look askance if you stuffed their tins with bloodworms. They might get their own back, though, by pinning a dead gudgeon to your lapel.

Casters might be classed as floating currency unless you anticipated the swing and stuck a dust shot to each of their little bums. And gozzers which survived the hazards of your back pocket might suddenly go downhill. Right down your trouser leg. And thereafter be fit for nowt. Or debased, as we say in the City.

So invest in nothing smaller than gilt-edged hooks, my boy, if you want to keep your currency stable.

But even hard currency is not one hundred per cent reliable. Top joints can develop a permanent set, even if you stick them down your wellie tops. And nobody wants to handle bent money.

Floats can be a positive hazard. Have you ever seen somebody with a porcupine quill in his trouser pocket forget that it's there and sit down quickly? Have you ever thought how much it costs to mend a bloke-sized hole in the ceiling?

Finally, let us all keep in mind the experience of the tackle dealer who opened a shop next door to a lunatic asylum.

The psychiatrist in charge of the asylum came round and said, 'When my patients come in to buy tackle, they'll try to pay you in milk-bottle tops. Don't say anything. Just take the bottle tops and I'll settle up with you at the end of the month.'

Sure enough, the lads from the loony bin came round, kitted themselves out with all sorts of expensive gear, bought gallons of maggots, pounds of groundbait, and paid for it all with milk-bottle tops.

At the end of the month the psychiatrist came into the shop.

'Any trouble with my lads?' he asked.

'None at all,' said the dealer. 'Perfect gentlemen. They spare no expense on the old tackle, though. I hope you don't get a shock when you hear how much the bill is.'

'I'm sure I won't,' said the psychiatrist. 'And it's been very good of you to take all those milk-bottle tops.'

'Don't mention it,' said the dealer. 'That will be £2,463·50.'

'Very reasonable indeed,' said the psychiatrist. 'Can you give me change for this dustbin lid?'

Where does it hurt?

This time the Parker Institute for the Study of Anglers' Nasties looks at anglers' injuries and their causes.

An injury is where the body has suffered some direct physical contact with a hostile body or object, where the flesh or bones have been bruised or broken. Being trodden on by a cow or bitten by a gudgeon are injuries.

Hooks in Funny Places

Hooks, single, double or treble, find their way into the most unlikely parts of the anatomy after an inexpert cast or after standing too close to an enthusiastic beginner.

Hooks in the backside can be diagnosed by the patient's refusal of a chair and the inability to stand still.

Hooks in the ear, especially with plugs attached, can be recognised instantly by the wearer's resemblance to David Bowie.

Care should be taken not to whip out the object without first making absolutely certain that you have the right one. The patient could be a Gipsy or seafaring man with one earring, and the hook stuck somewhere else.

Hooks in the nose can be traced by asking the patient, 'Do you always talk like that?'

If the answer is, 'Doe. Odly thinth I got thith flabid thig ub by dothe,' then you can be pretty sure where the trouble lithe. Sorry, lies.

Flattened Appendages

Anglers spend a lot of the time getting trodden on. Mainly by cows and bullocks. Bulls do not get the chance to tread on so many because the average angler, whatever his age or physical condition, is generally over the first fence as soon as identification is anywhere near positive.

But do not administer a foot-and-mouth injection without first being one hundred per cent sure of the cause of the injury. Anglers get trodden on by other things, too, More often than not, other anglers.

It happens frequently when a coach disgorges at a patchy water and a stampede starts for the best swims. Or when the coach stops at a pub with only five minutes left to closing time. Or in the rush for the bar when the match winner announces, 'The drinks are on me.'

Anglers also get trodden on by their wives, but this is dealt with in more detail under *The Battered Angler* (q.v.).

The Rod Rest Risk

Rod rests are among the most dangerous pieces of angling equipment, and often find their way into the angler instead of the bank.

For the benefit of non-angling doctors, a rod rest is a long, slim piece of metal, pointed at one end and v-shaped at the other. When one has penetrated deeply, the condition can be recognised by the fact that it is still sticking out of the angler when he arrives at the surgery.

Rod rests through the foot are the mark of an impatient angler. He has jabbed the rest into the bank without first ascertaining the location of his right wellie.

Rod rests in the rear are the mark of a careless angler. He has left it propped against his basket, sharp side up, and then sat down heavily.

Rod rests up the nose are often the mark of the excitable angler, generally of French, Italian, Spanish, Jewish or Pakistani extraction, who has gesticulated wildly to a mate without remembering what he had in his hand.

Not all these wounds, however, are self-inflicted. A closely-won match, a disagreement over the peg draw, allegations of malpractice, or arguments over who got to a swim first, can result in mass outbreaks of swordplay and their inevitable consequences.

The Battered Angler

The Battered Angler Syndrome is one of the sociological phenomena of our age. Since the advent of Women's Lib, more and more anglers' wives are questioning their husbands' God-given right to disappear for days at a time and come back unfit for human consumption.

Diagnosis is not at all difficult. As the Battered Angler has generally been subjected to a verbal, as well as physical assault, he often arrives at the surgery in a state of advanced deafness.

This can be ascertained quite quickly by asking, 'And how are we feeling today, then?' If he cups a shattered hand to his cauliflower ear and says, 'Yer what?', then you can be reasonably sure how he came by his injuries.

Talking about that . . . no, hey up—the wife's just come in. Hello, darling. Had a good day at the knacker's yard? Hey! No! Put me down! Gerroff! Do that just once more and I'll *scream* . . .

What's the Chinese for 'Sieg Heil'?

It is an unproven and wildly inaccurate fact that 50 million people are born into this world every day, one third of them Chinese.

To put it another way, if everybody in China were to start marching past you four abreast, making eight, they would never stop marching. The ones at the back would be breeding so fast that they would be queueing up to join in. After ninety years or so you would probably get tired and go home.

I am trying to get round to the subject of overcrowding in angling, and I am sorry I mentioned the Chinese, because they are not a problem on our canals. Though no doubt they are in China.

I should have started with the Japanese, whose shortage of angling waters is so acute that they fill up municipal swimming baths with fish on a Saturday night and all crowd round for an inscrutable oriental angle. The Japanese are not a problem on our canals either, come to think about it. So without more ado I shall get to the all-British heart of the matter.

Have you noticed, over the past few years, how many other people are fishing where once you never saw a soul all day? How there is always someone at your favourite pitch, no matter how early you get down there?

You can't blame the immigrants. Unless you count the Irish feller who cadged a hook, shot and a double handful of maggots from me on the Grand Union. This is a British problem and we have to tackle it in a truly British way. By cunning.

The average angler wants peace, quiet, solitude. If he doesn't get it, he'll move on. What you have to do to ensure your own peace, quiet and solitude is to make sure that nobody else gets any. (Eh, this is rotten, isn't it?')

Start by sitting close to the next bloke. So close that he can hear the irritating personal habits you have just developed. Suck noisily through your hollow tooth. Sniff up loudly and regularly. Clear your throat with a proper hrumph . . . hrumph . . . HARUMPHHH!

Whistle through your teeth. Tunelessly. Tap out a staccato and offbeat accompaniment with your fingers on the top of the bait tin.

Sing. Quietly and flatly. Some of the good old good ones. *Only A Rose. A Bird In A Gilded Cage. Come Into The Garden, Maud. My Yiddisher Momma. Who Hit Nellie In The Belly With A Barbel?*

If he stays put he must be tone deaf. Or just deaf. So stomp over heavily.

'Morning. Anything doing? No, I thought not. There's been nothing much caught round here since they dumped the cyanide. You can't lend me a maggot, can you? And a couple of worms? Will you be using all that bread? I did a silly thing this morning. Came out without the groundbait. You've got plenty there, I see . . .'

Generous soul that he is, he might load you up with maggots, worms, bread, groundbait, hooks, shot and a fill of baccy. In which case you will have to start the scratching routine.

Gently at first. On the back of the neck. Then under an armpit. Then both places at once. Suddenly you switch the scratching to the knees.

'Oh dear, the doctor warned me I was due for another dose of these. He reckons I picked them up in that Spanish prison when I was stranded after the international. Little devils, you can't see 'em and you can't get rid of 'em. You wouldn't like to scratch my back, would you?'

It is possible that he doesn't lose his nerve, even when faced with the dreaded Spanish invisible things, but gives you a scratch between the shoulder blades with a rod rest.

All that is left, as a last desperate throw, is the Third Reich Twitch.

Twitch mildly at first, and increase the severity and frequency as your monologue progresses.

'That doctor. Knows nothing, I tell you. Nothing! He spent hours yesterday telling me I was not Napoleon. I *know* I'm not Napoleon. My own retreat from Moscow was much better organised. And I was not retreating! I was advancing backwards merely to regroup. If Bormann had not left me in the lurch we would have swept back . . . swept back, I tell you!'

Finish by sticking your arm in the air and letting rip with a couple of *Sieg Heils*. If that doesn't shift him, nothing will.

*　　*　　*

It has just occurred to me that if this catches on, our canals could be lined with blokes sucking their teeth, sniffing up, clearing their throats, whistling tunelessly, singing flatly, borrowing shamelessly, scratching furiously, twitching madly and shouting *Sieg Heils* all over the place.

We might be better off with the Chinese.

That'll larn you

As you lay there, easing the splints and waiting for the stitches to be taken out, you could have been forgiven for thinking that there have been some rough old Nationals of recent years.

Rough my foot. They were nothing on the 1984 one. A report of which comes to you now by courtesy of the Petulengro Parker plastic ball.

Enough of this whining self pity. Just think yourself lucky. You're still breathing. Even though it is with difficulty. Now hear this.

Sludgethorpe, October 1984
From Our Own Reporter. Posthumously.

As firemen washed the blood from the towpath of the Brick Kiln Lane arm of the Sludgethorpe-Slagville canal, scene of unprecedented violence at the Division Sixty Three National, the big question still remained unanswered—Why Was This Allowed To Happen?

It remained unanswered because anybody asking it was escorted into a plain van and driven away.

A record number of anglers was disposed of by the stewards even before the match began. Seventy-two were disqualified for carrying unauthorised equipment, i.e. fishing rods. Fifty-nine were discovered carrying bait upon their persons. The team from Leicester were reported for asking the way and summarily executed. One-legged Seamus O'Toole, whose crutch broke down 36 miles from the venue, was told to hop it.

The rigid imposition of the rules continued on the bank, enforced by stewards trained in crowd control, Kung Fu, nostril-slitting and tupping and porring. Sludgethorpe ace Chalky White was taken away and beaten on the soles of the feet after being discovered eating a sardine butty. Four anglers using French roach poles were charged with treason and held until the Home Office could find somebody familiar with the techniques of drawing and quartering. Two Salford anglers were shot for coughing.

Perhaps the most unfortunate, judging by the noise he made, was John Thomas Dingling, the ace from Cockfosters, whose swingtip was confiscated.

'I kept telling them,' he said, his voice high-pitched with emotion, 'that it wasn't a swingtip at all.'

Forensic experts later confirmed that it was not, in fact, a swingtip, but for security reasons were unable to reveal its exact nature.

The three thousand anglers who were taken away by police at the request of the stewards were still helping enquiries late tonight.

'It'll take us a fortnight to duff this lot over and get the voluntary statements,' said Inspector Adolf Nark. 'We're only human, you know.'

At the final whistle the stewards—resplendent in their spiked boots, half-mast jeans and bomber jackets—escorted the remaining four anglers to the weigh-in. And what a finish.

The match was won by the Slagville Sticklebashers with a team aggregate of four drams. The highest individual weight would have been that of 97-year-old, partially-sighted lollipop man Albert Fluke . . . if his minnow had not flipped off the pan and been crushed under a steward's fighting clog.

There was no chance of a re-weigh because of the bits of turf and human flesh clinging to the remains of the fish. ('We're nothing if not fair,' said steward Heinrich 'Mad Titch' Grendel, as he smilingly broke the arm of the protesting Mr Fluke.)

The last word came from a spokesman for the National Association for the Abolition of Angling, speaking through a knothole in the double-locked doors of the HQ in Colditz Avenue, Smethwick.

'Say what you like. We've brought order and discipline back to match angling. The success of today's operation has given us all the encouragement we need to clamp down even harder at next year's National. We'll give 'em catching bloody fish . . . '

Lock up your daughters

The first month of the close season is time enough for the young angler's fancy to turn to thoughts of activities other than long trotting, stret pegging and skull dragging.

By the end of the month he has stopped dreaming of beating Benny Ashurst by a narrow 60 lb. of roach and bream, and started having visions which would cause Mrs W. some concern.

He has started wearing a tie at weekends, combing his hair and shaving. He has started noticing things like girls' eyes, thighs and well-rounded thingies.

And the single ones are worse.

Statistics show that the middle of April accounts for 87·5 per cent of proposals from anglers of marriageable age and status. Reasons for this include the facts that they are at a loose end, a low ebb, feel emotionally deprived and still have time to get the whole thing over with before the middle of June.

Mothers—look out of the window. Is there a moonstruck lad hanging around your gate, wearing a badge-covered bobbly hat, smelling of aftershave and old roach?

He's after your daughter, the rotten angling thing, he is. Get rid of him before it's too late. Throw something at him. The ironing board. The sofa. Grandad. The cat.

Tell the unsuspecting, innocent girl what it will mean if she swallows his line, succumbs to his blandishments, allows him to press his troth or plight his suit. Save her from a death worse than fate.

Tell her what it means to be an angler's wife. Tell her about:

The long, cosy, romantic chats. After the Epilogue or the late night horror movie. About how he had this roach beaten and nearly in the net when old Fred fell in, frightened it off the hook and lost him the match.

The Monday morning trail. Of odd socks, pullovers, wellies, string vests, baskets, half-empty bait tins . . . you name it. All through the house. None of which you must wash, burn, fumigate or throw away. But must collect with the reverence due to holy relics and put them all where he can find them, without opening his eyes, next Saturday morning.

The weekends. The long, glorious, sun-drenched weekends of early summer. On which he is considerate enough to leave you free to do the decorating, plumbing, carpet laying, or to watch the telly right through to the national anthem on Sunday night. About which time you hear his familiar footsteps crashing through the milk bottles and his husky, manly tones enquiring, 'Who the bloody 'ell put them things right where I'd fall over em?'

The friends. The sophisticated, intellectual coterie which gathers naturally around a man of action, personality, intelligence and wit. Paddling into your kitchen, the floor of which you have just washed. Bearing pipkins, popkins, pupkins, crates, barrels and bottles. So enraptured by your hospitality that half of them are still there next morning, spark out among the empties. Having thoughtfully tucked behind the sofa cushions the odd, unclaimed, but un-questionably dead, pike.

The love life. Intensive. Passionate. Demanding. All the way from mid-March to mid-June. After which he has to save his strength for the elimination matches to make sure he gets into the club's 'A' team.

Tell her. Openly. Frankly. Honestly. As mother to daughter. If she won't listen, or the lad at the gate won't take the hint after having the cat wrapped round his neck and the poker bent over his bobbly hat, lock her upstairs until June 16. Or put her name down for a short-term commission at the local nunnery.

... being extracts from the diaries and other documents of the Sludgethorpe Waltonians. This from the diary of Vera, long-suffering wife of Harry Turner.

I'm very worried about Harry ...

It's always the same with Harry at this time of the year.

'Three months,' he keeps saying. 'Three bloody months. Nobody needs that long. I wouldn't care if their sex life was anything to write home about.'

(When we first got married, I used to wonder what he was talking about—my mother had always maintained that he wasn't all there—but gradually I realised that he was going on about the coarse fishing close season.)

Then he gets one of his moods on and goes out to *The Bricklayer's Arms*, *The Hangman's Noose* or the *Cock and Bottle*, depending on which landlord is still speaking to him.

If his mood is still on him when he gets back, he kicks the cat and clouts our Jason. And tells Jason he should be down the pits at his age instead of loafing about and twanging his guitar.

It's not too bad if he's met Horace Harris or Chukkitan Chansit, his little Pakistani mate from work. They generally cheer him up a bit. I hope Harry's not being a bad influence on Chuck. He's always been a nice lad (Chuck, not Harry). But when they came home the other night from the *Bricklayer's*, Chuck was singing something about *Aunty Mary had a canary up the leg of her drawers* and tried to tell me a story about a commercial traveller who had to sleep on a billiard table.

In the main, though, Harry is very down. Even his ferret doesn't seem to be much consolation. All I can hope now is that the wormarium he is building at the back will take him out of himself.

Mind you, it's an eyesore, that wormarium. Harry says he's designed it on thoroughly proven scientific and ecological principles, but to me it's just a pile of old sacks and tea-leaves. And it doesn't half smell.

The close season does have its compensations for me. I do see Harry at weekends. He's either grumbling or sleeping, but at least he's there, bless him. I don't open the fridge to find it stacked with tins of maggots, or open the bread bin to find that he's gone off with my two fresh loaves, or start to bake and discover that he's used all the flour in the groundbait. Best of all, for three whole months I can use my mincer without worrying whether Harry's cleaned it properly after putting a load of worms through it.

I've been able to give his fishing outfit its annual tubbing. The trousers were so stiff with dried mud, slime and heaven knows what else, that I had to crack them with the toffee hammer to get them into the washer.

I had to throw away his seaboot stockings that he wears inside his wellingtons. I'll be in trouble when Harry finds out because they were his lucky socks—he was wearing them when he won one of the Waltonians' elimination matches. But what use they are to him without toes and heels, I can't think.

And the things I found in his anorak pockets. There was a hard, green, mouldy thing that turned out to be the crust of a veal and ham pie he took with him last October, three half bottles of Scotch (empty), a bobbly hat he's been looking for since Christmas, an IOU for five pints of bitter from Horace, a chunk of rockhard cheese, nine disgorgers, seventeen floats, two tins of split shot, enough raffle tickets to paper a wall, three bottle openers and a pile of ferret droppings.

Mind you, that cheered him up a bit. He took the whole lot into his shed to play with. He's in there now, bless him, singing at the top of his voice, 'Memories are made of this . . . '

Love a duck

Eyes down, folks, and let's have your attention, please. For National Love A Duck Week.

I have initiated Love A Duck Week to focus attention on one of the really underprivileged members of our society, one of the victims of the class system, one of the unsung heroes of our parks and countryside.

Remember that British ducks fought alongside us in two world wars. Are we now to cast them off, like sweaty socks, in their hour of need?

Never. The slogan for National Love a Duck Week, folks, for everybody, is LOVE A LICKLE DUCK A DAY.

Seriously, ducks don't have much going for them. They're little, for a start, on little legs. I wouldn't fancy being a duck with a touch of ground frost about. And the funny way they walk. As if they've got duck's disease or something.

They're not all that pretty. They've got cute faces, but daft ones. Nobody ever writes an ode to a duck, or gets inspired to write songs about them. Duck. It's such a stupid name for one thing. It doesn't even rhyme with much that's printable.

A duck is really a deep thinker. But its vocabulary is limited. How can you stand up and make a public statement of policy, intent or philosophy when all that comes out is 'WAK'?

No country has ever taken up a duck as its national emblem. Can you imagine the American emblem if, instead of the eagle, they had Daffy Duck? I don't know, though . . .

You can't give ducks resounding names. How could you call them Galahad, Augustus, Julian or Parsifal? Or Fiona, Brunnhilde or Ariadne? No. Ducks are Freds, Jims, Willies, Cyrils; Florries, Lizzies and Ethels.

They're working-class, are ducks. They're one of us, brother. I mean, you can imagine a duck in a flat 'at—but in a topper?

And look how hard a duck has to work. Compare a duck egg with the size of a duck. It's much bigger in proportion than a hen egg is to a hen, or a swan egg to a swan.

That's why hens can part with an egg with a quick, 'Buk-buk-bawrk!' Why a swan can do it in haughty and abstracted silence. But why a duck mutters through clenched beak, 'Oh, my gawd . . . ' and breaks into a cold sweat.

Doesn't it ever worry you, the things that people do to ducks? Notice, round about Christmas time, how the park lakes get to look a bit underpopulated? I wouldn't care, but there's never enough on a duck to make a decent meal. And those flat ducks in the windows of Chinese restaurants, spread out like kippers in a row. It's still a mystery to me how they get like that. I've a theory that in Hong Kong they have regular duck-stomping ceremonies with massed Chinese feet in massed Chinese clogs.

OK, OK. So why should *you* be so fond of ducks? Because of their nice natures, that's why.

Admittedly, they'll come pestering for bread when you're trying to fish. But they'll clear off once they've copped a couple of crusts. Not like swans, which will keep coming back for more and turn nasty when they don't get it.

And they're friendly. Which counts for a lot in this cold, hard world. They'll come and sit down to watch you fish, and make drowsy little wakking noises. Once they're used to you, they'll let you stroke them and scratch their flat little heads.

They're much brighter than hens. I mean, you can talk to a duck and get some sense out of it. And they're much more relaxing. A hen is forever clucking and bobbing and twitching and wandering off, but a duck will sit there enraptured for hours while you give it the benefit of a lifetime's experience and philosophy.

Mad Mac spent a lot of time talking to ducks. He even bought a duck call so that he could really converse.

He said to the policeman who took him away, 'What's wrong with having a nice cosy quack with my little friends?'

'Nothing at all,' said the policeman. 'But not in the middle of Hemel Hempstead at half past two in the morning.'

That's the fuzz for you. No soul.

After this, folks, I hope that all of you will help to redress the balance, help to make life a little easier for the little quackers, by doing your bit for National Love A Duck Week. Take some extra bread down to the river. Spare the time for a scratch and a few kind words.

Always remember: a duck may be just a duck to you, but to some other little duck . . . she's mother.

Reservoir ears and nightfisher's nose

In dealing with anglers' afflictions, as the Parker Institute for the Study of Anglers' Nasties now proposes to do, we are in the middle mist area of conventional medicine. Some afflictions can stem from injuries; others can pave the way for infection and turn into diseases.

First, the definition. An affliction is occasioned by changes in the body temperature or chemistry as a direct result of contact with the elements. There may be also permanent or temporary structural changes.

Let us kick off, as it were, with one of the good old good ones.

Reservoir Ears

Reservoir bank anglers—or at least those who reckon to know where they're at—fish into the wind. Which is nice and pleasant in the summer. Keeps the flies off for one thing, and ensures a plentiful supply of God's good air.

But in the winter. My life. Several months of facing a Force Nine gale—with all that it brings with it in the way of rain, hail, sleet, snow, clapped-out migratory birds and falling branches—can do dreadful things to the old sticky-out bits.

First, they contract. It's a great cure for anyone with jug handles and a lot cheaper than plastic surgery, though it hurts a bit more. The contraction, though frightening to the uninitiated, is to be welcomed: if they didn't do it, the owner would be in grave danger of taking off.

Then they turn blue. It's not all that noticeable because by this time the nose has gone the same colour (see *Nightfisher's Nose*).

After that—and here's the rub—they turn back to front. It is Nature's way of ensuring the survival of the species, and would be ideal if all of us spent our time fishing into the wind or walking backwards. But when the angler leaves the reservoir and rejoins normal society, he gets funny looks.

'Mam! Mam! Mam! Why are that man's ears turned back to front?'

'Shut up or you'll get no tea. He might hear you!'

'He can't, mam. His ears are turned back to—ouch! What was that for?'

There are two possible cures for the condition. One is for the sufferer to sit for at least three months with the wind behind him. Gradually and imperceptibly the ears will turn the right way round. This is the recommended method from the point of view of permanence, lack of pain and long-term social rehabilitation. You will then have to treat him only for deep-frozen kidneys.

The quicker way, the instant cure, is for you to stand facing him and, holding your arms straight out in front of you, parallel to the ground, to take hold of an ear very firmly in each hand. Then ask him, on the command 'Hup!' to do a quick back flip.

As soon as he has stopped screaming he will be delighted to find that his ears, if they haven't come off in your hands, are now the right way round. But he must be warned. This is by no means a permanent cure unless he takes strict precautions.

Firstly, he must give up reservoir fishing until June at the earliest. Secondly, he must put his ears in curlers every night, after first spraying them with aerosol ear-setting lotion and affixing them firmly to the sides of his head with contact adhesive or panel pins. If he doesn't he will wake up one morning to find them back to front again, and he'll have you up before the disciplinary committee for negligence.

Nightfisher's Nose

Though often found in tandem with Reservoir Ears, Nightfisher's Nose has a much wider range, can affect anglers on almost any type of water and, in spite of its name, at any time of the day or night.

An early symptom is the change of the epidermal hue to a bright cherry red. Often this is welcomed by unsuspecting nightfishers whose batteries have given out, because it helps them find their way in the dark.

Alas, this first symptom is swiftly followed by a steady secretion of sinusoidal fluid, which increases in volume from the classical dew-drop to a steady drip and then to a veritable torrent. This last condition is known as the Silversleeve Syndrome.

Worse is to come. The nose turns purple, then to a deep shade of ultramarine. And then it drops off.

Anglers should be advised to bring a detached nose with them to the surgery. Provided it has not been too heavily frosted, it can be sewn on again. Take great care to ensure that the nose is sewn on the right way up: the malformations of the nose peculiar to winter anglers often make it difficult to ascertain its original orientation.

One of the medical curiosities of this century was Mr Fred 'Hooter' Broadbottom, of Ardwick Green, upon whom an early nasal re-instatement operation was carried out in 1926. The nose was, unfortunately, replaced upside down.

From then on, every time he sneezed, his cap blew off.

A hell of a way to go

The Battered Husband Syndrome, described in an issue of the *British Clinical Journal*, made frightening reading.

The author was disturbed by the way a lot of husbands, who spend their working week in sedentary office jobs, 'launch at weekends into wild uncharted seas of manual labour and active pursuits'.

'The unskilled in perilous pursuit of the unusable', is how he described the activities of these poor lads. Doing things like digging the garden, cutting the grass, weeding, servicing the car, chopping wood, building bookcases, hanging wallpaper, laying bricks and painting things.

The injury rate, apparently, is alarming. And the nature of the injuries from hammers, axes, saws and dangerous things like that, horrifying. Cracked ribs, broken limbs, cut shins, aches and pains in the back and arms. To name but a few. Not to mention what happened to husbands like the noble loony who tried to paint a wall while standing on a tea trolley.

Those husbands who stop doing good works and turn to active sports involving balls—football, cricket, golf and hockey—do not seem to fare much better. They have a tendency, apparently, to stop 'these missiles with the bare hands, or with their heads, or their knees or their genitals'.

Nasty.

Those whose injuries are not severe enough to warrant a trip to hospital just can't wait for Monday morning when they can get back to work and away from it all.

'Now see how lucky you are,' tell the wife, 'to have a husband who puts the welfare of the family first and does not indulge in these dangerous pursuits. Who instead, out of pure consideration for his Nearest and Dearest, takes himself off to the peace and safety of the river bank.'

No matter how much you long to push a mower, pick up a trowel, saw, chisel or paintbrush, you fight down the impulse for the sake of the family. As breadwinner, you could not possibly risk falling off a speeding tea trolley or stopping a cricket ball with your thingies. (Knees and that. See above.)

No. It is a tribute to your selflessness, your lofty ideals, your innate capacity for self-sacrifice, that you deny yourself these pleasures. And instead spend the weekend in quiet and solitude, preserving your mind, body and knees for the weekly struggle to wrest a modest crust from the flinthearted employers of the Concrete Jungle.

Eh, lads, you should be proud of yourselves.

There was once an advert for an insurance company under the heading 'The Great Lover'. Which showed a little, bald-headed bespectacled twit, brandishing an insurance policy and surrounded by his adoring family. He *cared*, you see. What the advert didn't stress was that the poor bloke had to pop his clogs before they could collect.

You, I would respectfully submit, are the new breed of Great Lovers. By clearing off for a quiet dangle every weekend, by keeping away from serious injury or sudden death, you are ensuring your continued survival and earning capacity.

In years to come, when you are sitting in front of the telly, still sound in wind and knees, with the plaster falling off the walls, the roof caving in, the car rusting away on blocks in the garage, and the grass blocking the light from the windows, your adoring family will look at you and say, 'Dear Papa . . . he did it all for us.'

Or something like that.

Pith is a four-letter word

Still they come. Complaints about the bad language used by anglers. It's about bloody time something was done about it.

We must first admit that a certain amount of cursing is necessary in a sport like angling. Having a bit of a swear eases the pain, the misery, the tension, saves you throwing things at policemen, belting the wife or drowning the cat.

But there's no need to use naughty words. It's never what you say, it's the way that you say it. As they say.

So listen. To the Patented Parker Programme of Naughty Words for Gentlefolk. Comprehensive Cusses for Every Occasion. Guaranteed to Raise Nary a Blush on the Cheeks of the Most Maidenly.

Curses for the Nobly Born

Almost everybody in the country can trace his descent back to Henry VIII. He covered a lot of ground in his time. And that before the invention of the bicycle. So let's start with some Upper Class Curses.

True members of the aristocracy start with the advantage of a larger hooter and receding chin, both of which are invaluable aids to resonance. But don't worry. Just do your best, chin tucked in and hooter resounding, with:

Gad!

I say!

'Pon may soul!

Really! (pron. *Rahlly!*)

What, what, what! (pron. *Whaw, whaw, whaw!*)

Nice Words which Sound Naughty

There are any number of innocent words which sound really wicked. Try some of these. Definitions are included to save Mrs Thingy the trouble of looking them up:

Bolas! (A device made from strips of rawhide and three stone balls, if you'll pardon the expression, used by gauchos for tripping up cows, if you'll pardon the expression.)

Buckram! (A kind of coarse cloth)

Hawse holes! (Openings in the sides of ships to receive mooring cables)

Kakapo! (The New Zealand owl-parrot)

Kanakas! (A race of gentlemen from the South Seas)

Rowlocks! (Attachments on the sides of rowing boats to receive the oars)

Naughty Words for the Linguist

Anything said in German sounds (a) angry and (b) filthy. By the time you've told a girl you love her—*Ich liebe dich!*—she's been frightened out of her mind and sprayed from top to bottom. Try:

Baskenmutze! (Beret)

Fuchsteufelswild! (Very angry)

Schnattergans! (Chatterbox)

Schmuckstück! (Ornament, jewellery)

And how about the old German world for tank? My spelling might be off after all these years, but it went something like:

Schutzengrabenvernichtungspanzerkraftwagen.

No wonder they lost.

Anything said in a Scottish accent, especially a Glasga' one, also sounds quite horrifying. And some of the words, like *gralloch* and *pibroch*, are quite revolting. Because my path through life is beset by wandering Jocks, and because I wish to keep my lum as lang as there's a reek left in it, I will say no more.

Naughty Sounding Angling Phrases

What need have we of borrowing when there is such a splendid vocabulary of English angling phrases to choose from? Who could take offence, or who could not take offence, at such magnificent expletives as:

Anatto me gentles!
Riddle me casters!
Dap me buzzers!
Dibble me droppers!
Pickle me pollacks!

And finally, the Big One, to be used in circumstances only of the most extreme annoyance and provocation:

Boiled brains and bullock's pith!

Hey, that's enough, Parker. Tek him off, lads, and wash his mouth out with Guinness. You ... you ... you dirty old angler, you!

Eyes down looking

There we were, around the table after the Sunday evening meal, all dopy and blissful after Dearly Beloved's superb spread.

From the telly, after a strangulated bit of tenor from one of the Stars on Sunday, came a smooth voice talking about heaven.

'What's your idea of heaven, daddy?' asked Darling Daughter.

I had to watch this one. When Darling Daughter calls me 'daddy' instead of 'dad', she is up to something. Probably trying to trap me into an answer like, 'Being locked in a pub with Brigitte Bardot for ever and ever.'

Play it crafty, I thought.

'My idea of heaven, Darling Daughter, would be to sit on a little pink cloud for all eternity, gazing into your mother's beautiful blue eyes.'

How *about* that?

'Play it again, Sam,' said Blue Eyes. 'They're green.'

My God, so they are. After all these years. Mind you, I'd thought that mine were green, but they turn out to be blue. A bit bloodshot round the edges, but still blue.

This I pointed out to Dearly Beloved, but it did me no good. I still had to wash the pots while the kinds danced round singing:

Doo-doo-deedoo-doo,
Daddy made a boo-boo . . .

In case you're wondering where fish come into this, I'll tell you. It occurred to me while I was doing penance that perhaps we look at fish as closely as we look at our wives. And that perhaps we are missing a lot.

Before you unhook the next fish, look into its eyes. (OK, unless it's a pike, you've got to look into them one at a time, but you know what I mean.) When you've done it, you'll find yourself taking the hook out ever so gently.

We'll start with the roach and get her out of the way because, lovely though she is, her eyes are the least impressive. Gentle eyes, modest and unassuming, but not much else. Like the eyes of the faded daughters of the clergy or the military, who finish up running Olde English Tea Shoppes.

The bream has eyes that are sort of soft and sort of dopy. Like the girls who used to line the wall at the Palais and—in reply to your sophisticated opener of, 'Do you come here often?'—would reply, 'Yer . . .'

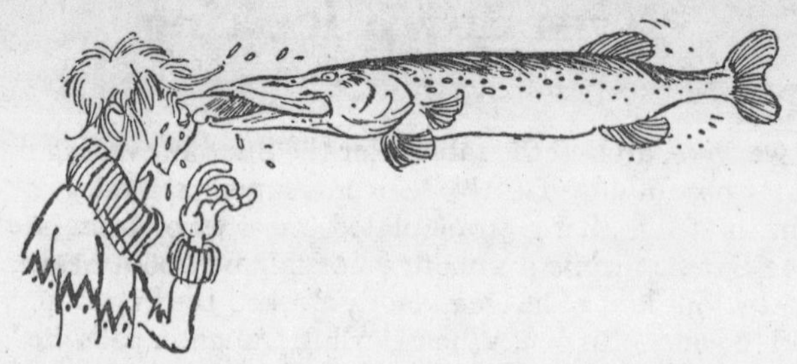

The gudgeon has eyes that are soft and warm, gently smouldering with a hint of restrained passion. If you met a girl at the Palais with gudgeon eyes, you knew that she would finish her chips quickly to make time for five minutes round the back.

(With your permission I'll drop the Palais before I get into any more trouble.)

Perch eyes are bold, brassy, indignant and challenging, saying, 'If I were four feet longer, I'd bite your bloody leg off—right up to your flaming ears!'

Chub eyes are hard and stubborn, like those of a Yorkshireman who is being badgered to pay his round, but who is standing there sullen and saying nowt. (Yorkshire readers over twelve stone and with any skill in the noble arts of self defence or clog fighting, please read 'Lancastrian' for 'Yorkshireman'.)

The tench has the African gold eye of the toad who turned into a prince after the beautiful princess had let him sleep on her pillow all night. But he doesn't have the same luck. There is not a single recorded instance of a tench shacking up with a princess.

(Remember the story of the toad who was still a toad next morning? The princess said, 'But you promised to turn into a prince'. 'Just shows you, darlin',' said the toad. 'Some birds will believe anything.')

The eel has small, glowing ruby eyes, set in the most delicately featured face. Neither face nor eyes get looked at while the poor old thing is being bashed, hacked and stomped on. Being an eel is not much fun.

The pike. When he comes to the top those eyes frighten you to death. But look at them properly. You might see what T. H. White saw and recorded in the magical book, *The Once and Future King* . . . 'his great jewel of an eye was that of a stricken deer, large, fearful and full of griefs'.

It is, too. And the discovery is one of angling's deep and lasting revelations.

Only mind your fingers.

SingalongaParker

In response to many requests from Mad Mac and Big McGinty, and ignoring the rude remarks from everybody else, I have researched a collection of old angling songs which were later rewritten by Tin Pan Alley and turned into chart-toppers.

One of the biggest surprises was to discover that the Israeli folk song *Hav'a Nagila* was originally the spiel of a Jewish bait salesman on Blackpool North Pier:

> *Have an*
> *Old peeler:*
> *Have two*
> *Old peelers:*
> *Have three*
> *Old peelers:*
> *Four bob*
> *To you . . .*

Remember the old Al Jolson song, *I want a Girl?* That was originally written by a lad whose father was a bit careless disgorging a 17-lb. pike:

> *I want a pike*
> *Just like the pike*
> *That bit*
> *My dear old dad . . .*

The *Anniversary Song* which Al made famous was adapted from *The Angler's Honeymoon*:

> *Oh . . .*
> *How we fished*
> *On the night*
> *We were wed.*
> *We fished*
> *And we fished*
> *While they mended*
> *The bed.*

Jerome Kern made a bob or two by adapting an old song about

the River Ouzel, in Bedfordshire, renowned for its lack of fish. The original, *Old Man Ouzel*, went something like:

> *Crazy anglers*
> *Fish de Ribber Ouzel*
> *Fishin' all day while de sane folk stay*
> *Roun' de corner*
> *On de ol' Gran' Union.*
> *Gudgeon bashin'*
> *Till de Judgement Day*
>
> *Don' look up*
> *An' don' look down*
> *Don' dare make*
> *Dat bailiff frown*
> *Change dat bait*
> *Weep an' wail*
> *Fergit yo' card*
> *An' yo' land in Jai-ail . . .*

Lastly, that robust old song from the days of the angling music hall, *Never Let Your Dingle Dangle*. A dingle, of course, being the extra-long fur-lined tie worn to protect a night-fisher's chest:

> *Never let your dingle dangle*
> *When you're out with the lads*
> *For an angle*
> *'Cos a pike on the rise*
> *Could bring tears to your eyes*
> *So never let your dingle dangle . . .*

... being extracts from the diaries and other documents of the Sludgethorpe Waltonians. This from a school essay by Jason Turner, Junior Member and son of Harry.

My old man

I like going fishing with my dad because he's such an old twit.

If it wasn't for me, he'd never get to the water. When the alarm goes off, he bangs on the bedroom wall and groans, 'Cuppa tea . . . ' By the time I've made it, he's gone to sleep again and I have to shake him very hard.

This wakes my mam up and she bashes him. I like that bit.

I get all the gear together and make the butties. It's no use leaving it to him. Last year we drove thirty miles to the river and he'd forgotten the rods.

Sometimes we walk down to the canal, but sometimes we go in the car to this river in the country.

I like the drive. We've got this old banger that hasn't got the strength to bang. It sort of wheezes. And every time somebody overtakes us, dad calls him all sorts of names.

When we get home, I like getting dad into bother by telling mam what he called the other drivers.

At the river we have to climb over a stile. Dad always tells me the same thing, about when he was in the army he used to jump over stiles like that carrying 80 lbs of equipment and a bren gun.

Then he climbs to the top of the stile, trips over his wellies and falls flat on his face. When he was in the army he must have been better at it.

He's very proud of his wellies because he's had them for 20 years.

'Fantastic grip these soles have got,' he said once. 'You could walk up a brick wall in them.'

That was just before he slipped on a cowpat. 'Careful on the brick walls, dad,' I said. He clouted me.

I got my own back later on when he waded in to pick up some freshwater mussels. I didn't tell him about the big hole in one of his wellies where the rubber had perished. The look on his face when the wellies filled up. I wish mam had been there. She'd have enjoyed it. And she might have stopped him clouting me again.

So we tackle up and get settled down. Dad always pinches the best looking swims for himself. Then he gets annoyed when I start catching fish and he doesn't.

He's always lecturing me on the correct way to play a fish and how to use the landing net. As soon as I get one he yells, 'Rod up! Don't panic!', comes charging across with the net, slips down the bank and sploshes it right on top of the fish. I lose more fish that way . . .

He is very safety conscious, is my dad. He has been ever since I fell in as a nipper and he took me home to mam all wet and sniffling. She didn't half give him the rounds of the kitchen.

So now, whenever we're walking along the bank, he keeps saying, 'Watch where you're putting your feet. Don't get too near the edge. Keep your eyes open for those holes . . . '

He was saying that once when he stepped in a hole and fell in. It was a scream that was. I took him home to mam, all wet and sniffling. She didn't half give him the rounds of the kitchen.

When the pubs open the fish stop biting. That's what my dad says, anyway. I don't see how he works this out, because mine don't stop and he generally hasn't had a bite anyway.

I don't mind this, really, because I can sit in the pub garden with crisps and a dandelion and burdock while dad tells all his mates what a great morning's fishing he's had.

I do very well out of this. If I don't split on him to his mates, I get another packet of crisps. And if I promise not to tell mam how many pints he's had, I get a ham roll.

He's not bad, my dad. For an old twit.

Eeny, Meeny, Miny, Fred and Bumface

You, too, can study aquatic life in the comfort of your own back garden. Watch fish, frogs, snails, beetles, leeches and other revolting creatures doing their own things.

You can do it with the Parker Instant Two-Pond System, a method which has been tried and tested in my own back garden and which has given me hours of fun and enjoyment.

The first thing you need is a wooden beer barrel. Full. When you've emptied it, that's the fun and enjoyment over with.

What you do now is to saw the empty barrel in half, crossways. (I put the crossways bit in because there's bound to be some twit somewhere who would try to do it lengthways.) Then you dig two holes and bung one half barrel in each (open side up, for the benefit of that same lad). Chuck a couple of spadesful of soil in each.

Get some buckets of water from the canal, along with some representative samples of plant and animal life. Take out any old tins/bottles/boots/dead cats/bedsteads/bicycle frames and slosh the water into the barrels.

Once the water has settled, which seldom takes more than six months, you can stock the ponds with creatures of your choice.

My ponds were stocked last year with goldfish and tadpoles. Goldfish because every time Darling Daughter went to a school fete she came back with one of the damn things in a plastic bag. Tadpoles because I wanted to strike a blow for democracy and establish at least one working-class pond.

This, I thought, would provide the opportunity for a detailed close-quarter study of the habits of tadpoles and goldfish. It did. And of the habits of starlings and pussycats. And it put me off Nature for good.

The little tadpoles in Pond Number One messed about happily until they became teenagers and sprouted legs. With these little legs they hopped happily out of Pond Number One and went hoppity, hoppity, hop towards Pond Number Two. (Are you sitting comfortably?)

But between them and Pond Number Two were either the starlings that live under our eaves, or our tatty cat Jemima and her tattier boy friend from down the road. Known to his owners as Edward. Known to me as Bumface.

The starlings went peck, peck, peck, and with every peck a frog disappeared. Jemima and Bumface went splat, splat, splat with theirs paws, and with every splat a frog was left looking very, very flat.

Sometimes the frogs got a reprieve. When Jemima and Bumface were eating the starlings. And they went hoppity, hoppity, hop towards Pond Number Two and then sperlosh! into the water. Where waiting for them were four hungry goldfish. Eeny, Meeny, Miny and Fred (There weren't going to be no Mo).

Eventually all the little frogs disappeared, either pecked, splatted, gulped or plain absconded. Jemima and Bumface had to find something else to occupy their tiny minds. And that's how Eeny, Meeny, Miny and Fred got their come-uppance.

Moral Number One is that messing about with ponds is no occupation for anyone with a sensitive nature, although it is just about the only excuse for getting in a full barrel of beer without throwing a party.

Moral Number Two is that it's tough being a tadpole. And not much better being a goldfish or a starling. But it can be fun being a pussycat. Even if your name *is* Bumface.

One for the money, two for the show

I know a bloke who . . . well, no, I don't know him exactly, but Mad Mac does. Sort of. It's one of those stories. Who wins incredible amounts of money at golf by a sheer war of nerves.

He goes round the clubs and challenges the best players for really big stakes. 'I'll bet my car against your car. Or my house against your house. Or, if you're really chicken, let's just make it a straight thousand quid.'

By the time the ace player gets to the first tee, he's already fretting about what the wife will say if he loses. And by the time he comes to an eighteen-inch putt, he's in such a state of worriting and tremblement that he misses by a yard.

And all the time his rapidly fading morale is being undermined by a running commentary from the challenger: 'You've got a tricky one there. Lee Trevino had the same trouble last time we played. Missed it by a mile, poor old lad . . . '

I'm working on this war-of-nerves technique for an incredibly successful run of fishing matches. It won't be long now before my smiling, classical mush—frank, open, honest and fearless—is decorating the *Angling Times* front page under the heading HOW *DOES* HE DO IT?

You may already have heard some of the rumours. About the hours of training on a secret stretch of water, timed by seconds with stopwatches and guarded by a cordon of Matchicor gorillas.

About the secret bait, the Parker three-inch fluorescent ultrasonic maggot. Over which the fish knock hell out of each other to get there first.

About the Parker Finger and Thumb Fifty Yard Flick. With which the lad has taken lighted fags from his friends' mouths in pitch darkness in the yard of the *Queen and Cobbler*.

You may also have heard stories, told in hushed and awed whispers, of the Parker Curse, and of the dreadful fates which have overtaken the very few anglers who have ever won against him.

Like the Curse of Tutankhamun, it *can* be dismissed as a series of pure coincidences. But there is no escaping the fact that Ernie Juggins, ace matchman of Osmondthorpe, was chopped into four pieces by the last tram to run in Leeds. That 'Flash' Pitt, champion matchman of Leigh South for years, expired after getting a pig's trotter stuck in his throat at the celebration dinner. That Thermo Klein, the reservoir ace, was caught up with a passing water skier

and went four times round the circuit underwater before he was—all too late—cut loose. That Long Odds Hodgson, famous for backing himself to the limit, was ruined when the bookie stepped into a Chinese disappearing cabinet immediately after the match and vanished forever from human sight.

Soon you will be hearing stories of the arrival of Parker at the canal by gleaming white Rolls or private helicopter, and of the march down to the peg preceded by the pipes and drums of the Boggart Hole Clough British Legion.

(If you haven't got colour TV now, rush out and get a set in case you miss the live coverage.)

On your screen will appear Parker removing his sequined cloak, or having it removed by scantily clad female attendants. (Y'all right for that job, our Brenda? Go steady on the chips.) You will see him making sure that his Jackie Pallo bow is securely in place on his flowing Adrian Street hair before he does a couple of handstands and a scissors kick to limber up.

After the match you will see the victorious Parker do a lap of honour up and down the cut in his Rolls, throwing pennies to the hoarse and hysterical crowds. (Well, ha'pennies. Let's not go completely barmy.)

So it's all set, folks. There's only one small thing worrying me. What if I lose?

I'll have to put the cat in pawn again.

Touch of the master's hand

I've been having trouble again with Number One Son.

Thinks he knows it all. And that his old dad knows nowt.

Just because of an unfortunate and coincidental series of happenings in which my normally superlative fishing skill was not seen to its best advantage.

It started on the canal, where Number One Son was fishing with the sons of Big McGinty.

'What ho, lads!' I greeted them heartily.

'Oh, gawd,' said Number One Son. *Sotto voce*. Which is Italian for muttering and giving dirty looks.

When I picked myself up after tripping over the rod belonging to Young McGinty Number One (well, what a daft place to leave it), I noticed the float belonging to Young McGinty Number Two was bobbing. And that he was not paying attention.

Quick as a flash, propelled by lightning reflexes and whipcord muscles, I was over in one bound. Snatching the rod from the rest and striking all in the same movement.

'Nearly had him that time,' I beamed, handing the rod back to Young McGinty Number Two. He is better at knots than I am.

'When's your birthday, Uncle Clifford?' he asked.

'December.'

'What,' he asked coldly, 'do you reckon your chances are of reaching it?'

My little ego fraying a bit at the edges, I moved on to the Parker Number One Son.

'Go away,' he said.

'Ah, me old fruit. From the look of that keepnet, you're not doing as well as you might. Permit me to point the way to instant success with the Parker Patented Superstar Cast.'

Without more ado, and wresting the rod from his unskilled hands, I flicked the bait out in a mighty arc.

If the speeding barge had not shot from cover, intercepting the bait and snapping the line, everything would have been fine.

The skipper shouted some naughty words.

'And you!' was my defiant replication.

A few weeks later, Number One Son went down to the local aquadrome. Where, even with the master's hand to guide him, he had never hooked more than four fish on any one trip.

This time, all by himself, he pulled out eighteen beauties. Fourteen roach, three perch and a pike.

'That,' I said, 'is a tribute to the way you've been taught. Even when I'm not there you are fishing in a manner befitting the son of Angling's Number One—'

'Dad . . . '

'No, don't thank me, old fruit. Your success is thanks enough. I couldn't really take the credit. All I did was to point the way . . . '

'Dad . . . '

'Please. Don't embarrass me. Don't say another word.'

'Dad. There really is something I'd like to say.'

Dad's eyes down, coyly. A little embarrassed soft-shoe shuffling. A maidenly blush spreading over the old weatherbeaten cheeks.

'All right, then. But shucks . . . '

'Dad . . . Next time I go to the aquadrome, will you do me a great favour?'

'Anything me old fruit. Just name it.'

'Stay outside and play with the traffic.'

Wait till I see that Doctor Spock . . .

The Angler's Prayer

Lord,
I am sitting here,
In inclement weather
And conditions of
Great personal inconvenience,
For all sorts of reasons:
To get away from the fumes, the smoke, the noise,
The rat race, the boss, the bank manager, the tax inspector,
The wife, the kids, the mother-in-law,
But ostensibly to catch fish.

The fish are slow in coming.
Possibly because they have been annihilated
By the four tons of toxic rubbish
Dumped upriver
By the factory
Last Tuesday.

At the end of this day,
Having had nary a nibble,
And feeling at odds
With the world,
I shall stumble from the meadow
Into the shelter and warmth
Of a well-appointed
Hostelry.

There I shall sup
More than is good
For my health, pocket or equilibrium.
Telling the while,
To whomever will listen,
The most outrageous
And unprincipled
Variations on the truth.

After which,
Having been ejected
By a landlord
Who no longer loves me,

Either for my money
Or considerable personal charm,
I shall wend my weary way home,
Holding deep philosophical conversations
With passing tomcats, stray dogs,
Lamp posts and policemen,
None of whom have much sympathy
With the piscatorial ethos.

Meanwhile,
Back at the cottage small,
Will be waiting
The Little Woman,
Light of My Life and Moon of My Desire,
With a feast
Long since past
Its prime.

Armed as a shield maiden
Of old Teutonic legend,
With a hairy great rolling pin,
Lethal-looking poker,
Substantial tin tray,
Or any combination of these,
The Light of My Life
Will bend one or all
Over my
Already throbbing
Swede.

If this, Lord,
Is what fishing
Is all about,
I give up.

Never again.
Under any circumstances.
Nothing would tempt me.
Wild horses would not drag me.
I'd rather die.
So there.   Amen.

P.S. Could You please make it a bit warmer for the match on
Saturday?

... being occasional extracts from the diaries and other documents of the Sludgethorpe Waltonians. This from the pen of Cliff Parker, festival consultant, frog fancier and barefoot clog dancer.

Two thousand years of Sludgethorpe

Very shortly—this year, next year or possibly the year after—Sludgethorpe will be celebrating its long and turbulent history with a festival entitled *Two Thousand Years of Sludgethorpe*.

The history has been turbulent mainly because they have been trying to get the festival organised for the past two thousand years.

I was asked by Mr Wilfred Harbottle, Hon Chairman of the Sludgethorpe Waltonians, if I could do my bit by providing an outline of the significant events in the town's history, with special reference to the long tradition of fish and fishing in the area.

This I have done, after hours of research at the Museum.*

I discovered several possible origins for the name of the town, each connected with a significant point in its history—the history not only of Sludgethorpe, but of our own dear island and its peoples. I have therefore based my paper on these origins and related events, and am content to leave their final selection and use to the good taste and judgement of Mr Harbottle and his Festival Committee.

Origin: Roman
Name: SLUXDORUM

Named from the cry of the Standard Bearer of the XIVth Legion, who leapt into the river with the colours and leapt out again very smartly on the opposite bank shouting, 'Oi ve! Slux schmux!' (Which, roughly translated, means, 'Sod this for a game of soldiers!')

It should be explained at this point that the XIVth Legion—to you, the XIIIth—had been recruited around the shores of the Dead Sea in an attempt to relieve unemployment among local fishermen.

---

* The Museum Tavern. A lovely pub, bang opposite the British Museum. When you can get in, that is, for all the layabouts who are supposed to be doing research across the road.

The Legion followed the Standard Bearer to a man, and knocked hell out of Boadicea to a woman.

They settled the area, got a grant from the Beth Din, and stocked the Slux with gefilte fish. The fish died of asphyxia in less time than you can say, 'My life', leaving the poor lads out of work again and reduced to drawing the *dolurum*, the Roman equivalent of National Assistance.

Origin: Saxon
Name: SLEOARGHFORD

Sleoarghford, or Slurry Ford, was so named because of the slime-covered stones on which so many of the migrating Saxon war bands slipped, thus giving rise to many of the old Anglo-Saxon words we use to this day in impolite conversation.

The first Saxons to cross the river were led by Ethelred the Unsteady, known to his followers as the Venerable Mead. Halfway across, a shortsighted pike took a fancy to Ethelred's accoutrements, giving him the inspiration for his famous high-pitched battle cry which went something like: 'Blooooooooooooooooo-dyell!'

Origin: Celtic
Name: SHUILEDAUGH or SOSPANDARCH

So named from the saucepan shaped Bronze Age paddling pool where the Scots, Welsh and Irish armies linked up for a combined operation against the Saxons. The night before what should have been the decisive battle, the Celtic allies pooled their resources and caroused on a mixture of Guinness, Glenfiddich, John Jamieson, potheen, red biddy and surgical spirit.

Next morning every man jack of them was found as dead as a doornail. On the frozen face of each man was a big, fat, soppy smile.

Legend has it that it was not the booze which did for them, but a surfeit of the local fish pie—known as Ruffe Duffe—which was peddled among the armies by Saxon secret agents and such of the locals who were short of a scilling or two.

Origin: Old Norse
Name: SLURPFJORD

Slurpfjord, meaning Slurp's Fjord, was named after the Viking sea wolf Slurp the Bandy, so called because of the revolting way he drank his soup and the funny way he walked.

Lonely for home, he said that Slurpfjord reminded him of Norway in the dead of winter.

'But Slurp, Leaper of the Waves and Plodger of the Pebble Strand,' cried Snorri Snottinose (official bard, toady and hired creep), 'that is in the middle of the six-month night when no man can see a hand before him!'

'Aye,' sighed Slurp, gazing around at the desolate scene, 'and would that it were still so.'

The first winter at Slurpfjord was a lonely one. The Saxons were so glad that someone had at last taken the place off their hands, that they left the Norsemen alone. The Vikings had no one to vike, and turned to fishing to remind them of the salmon and trout of their native fjord.

After a month of catching asthmatic gudgeon and wheezing bleak, and losing half a dozen berserkers through going around without their shirts in the fog, they packed up and went home, grounding the longship twice on the shallows of what is now Foundry Road Lock.

Origin: German
Name: SCHLUTZDORPF

Named after the 16th-century German alchemist Heironymus Schlutz, who fled to England to continue in secret his experiments to turn base carp into goldfish. After thirty years of trying, all he had to show for it was scales on his pestle and mud in his mortar.

He is remembered today, however, as the inventor of fish paste, the father of industrial pollution, and the founder of the chemical engineering industry which has reached its apotheosis in Sludgethorpe Plastics.

Origin: Low Dutch
Name: SLIJEDOORP

Named after Slije Tove and Sjuthat Doorp, the Dutch engineers brought over by William of Orange to drain the swamps after Mary had stepped in a puddle up to her muddle (as the Dutch used to call it) trying to do a Liz I on Willie's plastic mac.

After Tove and Doorp had spent ten years digging ditches, the swamps finally drained away. When they saw what was underneath they spent another ten years filling the ditches in again.

*   *   *

So there we are. Two Thousand Glorious Years. If there is one thing this investigation has shown, it is that a town like Sludgethorpe, however unprepossessing it may look, simply reeks. Of history?

Get your knickers off

It was a terrible blow to our British pride when the CIPS, the governing world match body, accused the National Federation of Anglers of double dealing.

They resurrected some old complaints about the 1966 world championship on the Thurne. When, according to Johs Kleinberg, the match committee secretary, 'The English gave visiting competitors nets with large meshes but used small nets themselves.'

I don't wonder the 1974 meeting on rule changes finished in a state of choss. Europeans we may be, but British we still are. They can't cast nasturtiums like that and get away with it. By Gad. And Rule Britannia! My life.

If they did get nets with large meshes—and I say if, brothers, only *if*—it was because of our British sense of decency and fair play. Paying these continental twits—pardon me—paying our European cousins a compliment, we assumed that they'd catch fish big enough not to go through the holes.

And as for us having small meshes, what the hell do they think we had left after we'd given them all the nice big ones? Not that I believe a word of it, anyway.

Now we get to the nasty bit. Seamy. Sordid. They'll have Missis Lighthouse after them if they're not careful.

'Some teams,' said Mister/Monsieur/Herr/Signor/Mynheer/Comrade Kleinberg (pick where you like; he was speaking for the lot of 'em), 'some teams were reduced to asking their ladies for their stockings in order to retain their fish safely.'

Ho, yes. A likely story. Pull the other one. It's got bells on.

'I'm terribly sorry, officer. A complete misunderstanding. I was only trying to get the lady's stockings off in order to retain my fish safely.'

Can you see us getting away with that? On the other hand, why shouldn't we? Make a change from dreary old fish.

This pair of tights, d'you see, Constable, is much more efficient than a stocking. Holds twice as many fish. Tench in the toes, carp in the calves, gudgeon in the gusset and bream round the bum.

* * *

I am using this bra, Inspector, only to strain my bloodworms.

* * *

These knickers tied to the rod rest, Superintendent, are purely for determining the strength and direction of the wind.

* * *

I requisitioned the garter, Your Worship, only because the elastic on my catapult broke.

* * *

The naked lady behind me on the bank, M'Lud, was a complete stranger. Judging by her accent she came from foreign parts. No, M'Lud, I've never been to Selly Oak in my life.

* * *

We wouldn't stand a chance, lads. Not a cat in hell's. But now we're Europeans we're as much entitled to try as the other lot.
So long as the wife understands.

Getting to the bottom of it

Of all the afflictions with which the Parker Institute for the Study of Anglers' Nasties has been called upon to deal, none has been so prevalent as the one most anglers hardly dare mention, let alone talk about.

Enough of this pussyfooting. Let's have it out in the open. We are talking, gentlemen, about (blush blush) piles. Which are nothing more than varicose veins of the bum. Situated, in darts terminology, round about the bull.

They are, as sufferers know too well, incredibly painful, and do not even have the doubtful compensation of being romantic. But they are certainly nothing to be ashamed of. Apart from the match anglers who are struck down by the dozen every season, lots of famous people have been afflicted.

Napoleon had them. That's why he had to keep saying, 'Not tonight, Josephine.' George II had them. He was, as we all know, the last English monarch to lead his troops into battle. After hours in the saddle at Dettingen in 1743 he slid from his horse and uttered the famous phrase (in German, of course, the natural language of the piles sufferer), 'Achtung! Donner und Blitzen! Sturm und Drang! Mein royalischen Bumm geblitzen ist!'

Hitler had them. He must have: he had everything else. Humphrey Bogart must have had them: that silent snarl with the top lip is one of the classic symptoms of the sudden twinge. Mad Mac and Big McGinty have them. And I've got them.

I don't believe there is a once-and-for-all cure, but I can offer one or two tips for easing the pain.

Firstly, keep the old appendage warm and dry. Use a cushion on top of your fishing basket. This helps also to keep at bay the other angler's curse, the dreaded Basket Bum.

Secondly, stop worrying. The things seem mainly to affect intelligent people like you and me, and to come on strong in times of mental and emotional stress.

Cut right down on the draught bitter. Either give it up altogether or switch to spirits. Neither solution is entirely satisfactory: one way you finish up miserable and the other way you finish up skint.

Cut out spicy foods. To a lover of curries and raw peppers, the future seems to hold nothing more exciting than black pudding and chips, but you find yourself in time appreciating the subtler flavours of gentle dishes like tripe stewed in milk.

An old country remedy suggested by an *Angling Times* reader—

sitting on a bucket filled with hay which has been sprinkled with eucalyptus oil and then soaked with boiling water—sounds promising.

But don't forget the water. Otherwise you could cop for a poultice of neat eucalyptus. Which would make you the first angler on Mars. Or you could drop a lighted fag end on the dry straw. Which would have the same result, but would make for a more spectacular trip. And which could get you mistaken for Halley's Comet by short-sighted astronomers.

You can buy tubes of stuff which you slap on the old bot. I used to keep a tube in the bathroom cabinet. I do so no longer, because one night I got home after a session with Mad Mac, cleaned my teeth and went to bed. Next morning, back in the bathroom, I'm shouting down to Dearly Beloved, 'Where's the toothpaste got to?'

'It's down here, love. We ran out, and I forgot to put the new tube in the bathroom.'

'Rubbish. I cleaned my teeth last night, so there must have been . . . Ooh . . . Oh 'eck . . . Yaaaaaaargh!'

It worked though. From that day to this I've never suffered with piles on my teeth.

As a last resort, of course, there's The Operation. Known in medical circles as Irish brain surgery. (Sorry, McGinty, ol' buddy. Only kidding. Kindly remove your fingers from my windpipe . . .)

The op is not a course I'm very keen on since I met

(a) A chap who'd had it, and whose affliction had reappeared in much more constricting surroundings and was consequently much more painful, and

(b) A doctor who told me that they save such ops for the end of the day because they let loose lots of 'orrible bacteria and they don't like infecting other patients.

So you get bunged in at eventide among all the other patients' germs while the nurses are sweeping away all the appendixes, gall-stones, legs and arms of the day's work. Charming.

But don't let it get you down, lads. It could be a lot worse. Remember the story of the ancient Chinese philosopher who thought he suffered from the old affliction. He thought about it for fifty years, and finally came to the conclusion that his navel, the seat of all wisdom, held the clue to the cure. So he got a screwdriver, put it in his navel, and started slowly unscrewing.

After ten minutes his bum fell off.

Boating is good for you

The river managers keep trying, bless 'em. To prove that heavy boat traffic improves angling waters.

And they're right, you know. If anything, they don't stress strongly enough the benefits to angling from the activities of those graceful craft and their handsome, high-minded skippers.

I have gone into it further for them. Scientific tests at the Parker Aquatic Research Laboratory and Chinese Takeaway have backed their claims to the hilt. And beyond. I offer the results of the research in case they need any more facts to help put those silly anglers in their place.

The bow waves of a boat undoubtedly oxygenate the water. As do hand grenades and sticks of gelignite. And by encouraging weak sections of the bank to collapse, they make an important contribution to the safety of anglers who otherwise might stand on them and fall in.

The waves also impart to keepnets that splendid side-to-side and up-and-down swishing motion so beneficial to captive fish, removing surplus slime and scales, trimming off overgrown fins, and ensuring a plentiful flow of oxygenated silt through the gills.

The movement of boats, four abreast at an optimum speed of 25 knots, rids the waters of all that dreadful old weed and the nasty creepy-crawlies which live in it. This ensures that none of our fish need worry about the problems of obesity in middle age.

Such weed clearance makes it difficult, if not impossible, for the fish to spawn, thus raising the high moral tone of underwater life. Striking a blow for standards of decency and respectability hitherto ignored by the loose-living creatures. All those gang bangs in the weedbeds. No wonder there were so many hybrids about.

The vast improvement of waters by regular boating is strikingly illustrated by comparing our waters with those of Ireland, where boating has yet to reach the English magnificence of scale. Just compare our lusty, healthy, grateful fish to the stunted, sickly specimens which are pulled out over there.

Both the food supply and environment in boating areas are improved no end by the by-products of boating which the generous sailors allow to flow without stint into the water. All that expensive oil and detergent, all those empty cornflake packets and buckets of slops, help to give the fish a plumpness and sheen unmatched in the western hemisphere.

All that splendid, selfless dredging which the authorities do to help

keep the boats moving. Without it we would find all our waterways
silted up as a result of the thoughtless pounding on the banks of
those millions of anglers' wellies. Do we ever find the boaters whining
and moaning about that? Do we ever see letters in the angling
Press from boaters whose craft have run aground, pleading for
anglers to fish in their socks?

And as for the myth about conflict between boaters and anglers.
Absolute nonsense. There has never been such a happy band of
brothers, embracing each other in fraternal greeting whenever they
meet. Those balls of groundbait, those handfuls of maggots, those
half bricks launched by catapult at the boaters, are the work of a
tiny minority of imported anarchists, students and yobboes, dedicated to the disruption of our society. It is their avowed aim, ladies
and gentlemen, to create a schism, cause bovver, start aggro,
between anglers and boaters.

And that would never do.

It comes to us all in the end

Having got rid of the old chestnut

> *Old anglers never die.*
> *They only smell that way.*

we can get on to the serious subject of Dead Anglers And What To Do With Them.

It is not a pleasant subject but, as the man said when he was hit from behind by a runaway tram, it comes to us all in the end.

The first thing to do when you come across what might be a dead angler is to make sure that (a) he is an angler, and (b) he is dead.

A live angler looks like an upright and mobile heap of rubbish in wellies. Therefore a horizontal and motionless heap of rubbish in wellies could very well be a dead angler.

Check further. Go through the pockets. If they contain only a pair of binoculars and a camera, he could be a birdwatcher or a dirty old man. If, however, they contain hooks, disgorgers, chunks of bread and cheese, links of sausage, slices of luncheon meat and a couple of dozen casters, he is possibly an angler.

Further investigation might reveal something gripped in the right hand: a rod, landing net or pint pot. If he still retains his grip on the pint pot, then he is not yet dead.

Let us now examine some basic resuscitation techniques. Speed is of the essence: you don't want to be hanging around on a damp bank all day. So try one or more of the following:

1. Remove his wellies and hold them under his nose.
2. Rush to the nearest pub and borrow the barman's apron. Just one smell of a barman's apron has been known to work miracles.
3. Whisper in his ear, 'What are you having?'. If this has no effect, shout, 'Last orders *please*!'
4. Shout, 'Hey up—here's the wife!'
5. Light a fire on top of him.

If these fail, you must now prepare for the Kiss of Life. To do this:

1. Lay him flat on his back.
2. Go through his pockets until you find his bottle of the hard stuff.
3. Take a stiff swig. Or two.
4. Find somebody less sensitive than yourself to do the kissing. Alternatively, borrow a vacuum cleaner or flag down a passing Sludge Gulper.

Anglers sometimes pass away in company, and this can be very embarrassing to their friends. People might think they're being stand-offish.

If an angler doesn't move in the pub when it's his turn to pay, he is either: (a) Forgetful, (b) Skint, (c) A Yorkshireman, (d) Dead. If:

(a) Jog his memory. With something heavy, or pointed. Or both.

(b) Have a whip round. But only on condition he gets his hand down first on the next trip out.

(c) Appeal to his finer feelings. After a count of ten, throw him out.

(d) Shove him under the seat until closing time. Leave five bob in his pocket for the cleaner.

If the angler is well and truly dead, his passing should be mourned by the club with suitable tributes. The following is a selection of tasteful epitaphs which can be used on the headstone:

Here lies Jim.
We do miss him
Now he's fished
To the end of the swim.

Here lies Cecil,
Best of the batch.
He heard the whistle
For the end of the match.

Here lies Fred,
Sadly dead.
In the ground,
Having missed his round.

Here lies Albert,
Clubman devout.
He had to go
When his ticket ran out.

Fit to drop

It comes to us all in the end. Age.

(Should have been a philosopher, this lad. Don't know how he does it.)

Not just age, but the failing of the powers and attributes that in our youth we took for granted. Rippling muscles, curly gipsy hair, hawklike eyes, flashing teeth. Me brother had those.

Came home to me suddenly. When I got a letter from the dentist saying can you come round for a look at your choppers. Alternatively, send them Recorded Delivery. And when I gave up my seat on the bus to this blonde with the long flowing hair. Failing to notice the tattoos, the beard and the sweat shirt stencilled Alabama State Prison.

Gad, I thought. The old powers of perception are not what they were. This finely tuned instrument, this perfectly formed body, is perhaps not what it was.

My duty was clear. To warn the others. Tell them how to make the most of what they've got while there's still time. Otherwise they may never land another fish. What's worse, may be carted from the bank slung under a landing net handle. And left outside the pub with rigor mortis setting in. While the other lads wait inside for the coach. With DTs setting in.

MAN! Do you want to be strong? Do you want to be mighty? Do you want the speed of a cheetah, the strength of a lion, the body of an Adonis?

Of course you bloody don't. What would you do with all that lot?

But you do want to get down to the river without having to stop for a cough every ten yards. You do want to distinguish a float from the rest of the rubbish on the surface without having to use a telescope. You do want to be able to distinguish the tremble in the line from the tremble in your knees.

So start before it's too late. Take up the Parker Look Younger, Live Longer and Be More Revolting Course.

Start with the teeth. Get them fixed. If you don't, you will not only be unable to cope with the cheese butties and bottle tops, but you may find yourself unable to bite through a line in under an hour. What's worse, be unable to pinch the shot on without swallowing enough lead to sink the mother-in-law. You'll get your real come-uppance on a fast and rising winter river. By the time you've gummed your way through half a dozen swan shot, it'll be summer again and the water will be down to the ducks' ankles.

The eyes are next. Get new specs by all means. But exercise the eyes as Nature meant you to. Stare at distant points of interest. Like those in the cheesecloth thingy across the road. They are even more interesting than floats. And come in pairs. One for each eye.

Get your proper sleep. In regular rest periods. After your tea. Even though the wife is dropping hints as subtle as sticking a paintbrush up your nose and putting a power drill through your pipe and slippers.

Avoid any possibility of physical injury. Keep away from ladders, saws, hammers, chisels and lawnmowers.

Keep your fingers supple and sensitive, as the classical violinists do. Never take up any implement which might impair these qualities. Such as a spade. And wear silk gloves when you eat your chips.

Drink plenty of draught bitter if you're to have your full quota of Vitamin B1, which is essential for the keeping at bay of night blindness and beri beri. On cold days chase it with something stronger to achieve the maximum peripheral vascular dilation.

Stick strictly to this regime, spartan and painful though it may be. And you, too, will stand a chance of winning the National at ninety-three. Fit, supple and hawk-eyed. Full of teeth and reflexes.

If the wife hasn't hit you first. During your evening rest period. With the lawnmower.

Wagstaffe bites yer legs

A disturbing thought, but apparently it's true. That football fans are deserting the game by the thousand and turning to angling.

While one can only marvel at their taste and discrimination, while one can only applaud the fact that they have seen the light, one must admit to a certain disquiet. One must. (End of Upper Class Twit phraseology.)

What's going to happen to the game? Not football. That will survive as long as three or four homicidal maniacs are able to gather together. Fishing.

Let us peer into the Petulengro Parker Plastic Ball and read the report of the Sludgethorpe–Slagville Derby Match of 1984.

From Our Own Reporter
Sludgethorpe, Saturday Night
Police with dogs were waiting at the Brick Kiln Lane depot as windowless buses arrived, packed with hatchet-wielding fans from Slagville. Several arrests were made and one or two duff-ups indulged in before the main body of Slagville supporters broke through the cordon and rampaged through Sludgethorpe.

Mr Edward ('Big Eddie') Fanshawe, 17-stone mine host of the *Bricklayer's Arms*, was taken to hospital suffering from cuts, bruises and a hatchet through the head after attempting to quell a disturbance in the saloon bar. His wife, 14-stone Jolly Alice Fanshawe, was about to be sedated when a stray brick saved the doctor the trouble.

Another public house, the *Hangman's Noose*, was burned to the ground in a mystery blaze, only 24 hours after the landlord, Mr Ebenezer Sackbutt, had taken out a £45,000 insurance policy.

'I am casting no aspersions,' said Mr Sackbutt, 'but it must have been those fiends from Slagville.'

Later a man, believed to be Mr Ebenezer Sackbutt, was helping police with their enquiries.

The entrances to Jackson's Clay Pit, venue for the big match, were sealed off by police with dogs and security men from the Honest Chalky White Matchicor Organisation as banner-waving fans from Slagville and Sludgethorpe fought to get in first.

There were chants of *I-van! I-van!* from the Slagville contingent. (Their top matchman, Ivan Chuckerbutty, was strongly fancied.) The Sludgethorpe fans charged with banners bearing the slogan, *'Wagstaffe Bites Yer Legs'*. (Norman Wagstaffe, the up-and-coming

White Hope of the Waltonians, had built up a reputation for dealing summarily with opponents who fancied their chances.)

The scenes at the pit, only minutes after the first whistle had gone, were chaotic. Sludgethorpe had won the toss and chosen to fish with the wind in their faces. The wind served only to add impetus to the flight of the toilet rolls thrown from the sunken crane by Slagville fans, who had paddled across on rafts improvised from party-size beer cans lashed together.

When the teams changed ends at half-time, there were ugly scenes as fans of both teams leapt at opposing competitors, slashing their nets and knotting their swingtips.

Serious fishing was held up throughout the match every time a fish was caught. No sooner was it unhooked and in the keepnet, than the captor was surrounded by his team mates, who kissed him and dribbled all down his ganzi. He then did a lap of honour around the pit, waving both arms and shouting, 'I Am The Greatest!'

Several matchmen got back to their pegs after the lap to find that opposition fans had cut their keepnets adrift or stolen the fish.

Five minutes before the final whistle was due, fans from both sides ran on to the bank and fraca'd about. Police with dogs and security men from the Honest Chalky White Matchicor Organisation moved in from each end of the pit to restore order, but finished up in a free fight with each other.

'It was their fault,' sobbed PC Genghis Himmler in an ambulance later. 'They trod on my poodle.'

'It was their fault,' said Mr Chalky White, head of Matchicor, in another ambulance. 'Them poodles was biting where they'd never been trained to.'

While all this was going on there was a mass streak by the Sludgethorpe and District League of Gentlewomen, in protest against the amount of violence in angling.

'Not a pretty sight,' said the vicar of Sludgethorpe St Longford's.

This evening questions were asked in the House about the upsurge of violence on the bank. Several motions were tabled, by all five members present, calling for the fencing in of match fishing fans and the bringing back of National Service, the cat, the rack, the thumbscrew, the treadmill, the iron maiden, the gallows and drawing and quartering.

The last word came from Cliff (The Mouth) Cluff, self-appointed oracle on all matters piscatorial, frog fancier, maggot breeder extraordinary, and barefoot clog dancer:

'Welllllll . . . Briannnnnn . . . '

And what more could one wish to say?

The Sludgethorpe Diaries

... being extracts from the diaries and other documents of the
Sludgethorpe Waltonians. This from the diary of Chukkitan
Chansit, the club's Pakistani member.

The good ship 'Venus'

The British are a seafaring nation, my good friend Harry Turner
is telling me.

I am telling him that nobody of my acquaintance in Sludgethorpe
seems ever to be faring the sea. Harry is telling me the names of
such people as Drake, Raleigh, Nelson, Frobisher and his Uncle
Willie from West Hartlepool, none of whom had any connection
with this esteemed town, famed originally for its engineering, but
now only for its plastics and its courageous but unsuccessful football team.

Tupper Brown is interrupting to say that if it were not for the
English seafarers, my people would never have been discovered. I
am replying that to my knowledge we were never lost, when Harry
is saying to be shutting the cakehole and forking out the money for
the fishing trip to be taken on the sea by the Waltonians.

*   *   *

We are travelling on the sharrybang to the sea, laden with lots of
crates for the bhoosing and singing jolly songs. These songs, Harry
is telling me, are of the English seafaring tradition, sung by the
sailors as they are maining the splicebrace and keelhauling the
barnacles.

Songs such as 'Yo-ho-ho And a Bottle of Rum' I can understand,
although fifteen men on a dead man's chest is seeming extremely
overcrowded, but I am being confused by other songs. One is con-
cerned with a wish to be rolling over in the clover, an occupation
which I could only envisage as being carried out on dry land, and
another with three German officers who are crossing a line for the
most extraordinary reasons.

Before I am able to question Harry about the significance of such
things, we are at the seaside and climbing into the vessel which is to
recapture for the Waltonians their seafaring heritage.

The vessel is bearing the name of *Venus*. Harry is finding this very amusing and is reciting a poem about a good ship of that name. He is overheard by the captain, called Skipper, who is looking very fierce and splendid in a cap with a badge.

This Mr Skipper is telling Mr Harbottle, our distinguished chairman, that he is wanting all his orders obeyed, and that he is wanting no nonsense from any of our members.

Hearing this, Harry is debating whether to be fetching Mr Skipper a punch up the throat, but Mr Harbottle is being most conciliatory and assuring Mr Skipper of our best attention and exemplary conduct at all times.

With this assurance, Mr Skipper is starting the engine and steering the boat away from the land. Everybody is singing more jolly seafaring songs and bhoosing merrily. This is lasting for about half an hour, by which time we are beyond the calm water and into some which is making the boat go up and down. Then there is a gradual lessening of the singing and also of the bhoosing, which is no doubt occasioned by the excitement of approaching the fish.

It is another hour, however, before the vessel is stopping. By this time there is complete silence from many of the members, some of whom are not looking well at all.

'Lines out!' Mr Skipper is shouting, and we are all throwing our lines over the side, first putting on the hooks some pieces of old fish which Mr Skipper has provided most thoughtfully in plastic buckets, these being no doubt a tribute to the native industry of Sludgethorpe.

We are waiting for a long time for something to happen to the lines. In the meantime, many of the members are turning the most peculiar colour of green, and leaning over the side in a state of apparent indisposition.

Harry is saying that I should be so lucky with a tan like mine because the green is not showing. I am saying that, although I do not come from a seafaring nation, I was having a very rough trip indeed to arrive in this country and have since been immune to all kinds of motion.

Suddenly my rod is bending and my reel is making screaming noises. I am winding in with the feeling of a very heavy creature on the line. This is not well received by members such as Clogger Sedgewick and Tupper Brown and others who are disciples of Mr Powell. They are looking at me most jealously and saying jammy black boogher.

Harry is saying, good lad, Chuck. Reel it in and let us be having the shufti (an Arabic word he learned when he was a very brave member of the British army).

Suddenly there is a very big splashing at the top of the water and I am looking at something most monstrous. I am feeling a very strong urge to be dropping my rod, but I am telling myself I must be brave, even though I am not coming from a seafaring nation.

This thing is looking very much like a snake, but very much thicker and with a large mouth full of teeth.

Harry is saying it is a gongher heel. I am thinking that I do not like this gongher heel very much, when Mr Skipper is leaning over the side with a large hook on a long pole and sticking this hook into the gongher. Now I am feeling sympathetic towards it, but when Mr Skipper is dropping it in the boat, I am once more not liking it.

It is wriggling and turning to bite the pole and everyone is rushing to be out of the way. Suddenly Harry is hitting it very hard with a piece of iron and then holding open a sack for Mr Skipper to drop it in.

Mr Skipper is saying he is glad to see that Harry is not so daft as he looks. Harry is offering him once more the punch up the throat, when our esteemed chairman, Mr Harbottle, is coming out from behind the mast where he was hiding away from the gongher.

He is saying that I am please to accept his congratulations and those of my fellow members, although Tupper Brown and Clogger Sedgewick are not looking with very congratulatory expressions.

There is no more time for congratulations, however, because suddenly other members are having the bites and the strikes. This time they are fishes of different shapes. One, lifted up by Tupper Brown, is said by Harry to be a pollack. The fish is releasing itself from the hook and falling back into the water.

Mr Harbottle is asking what has happened and I am saying that Tupper has dropped a pollack. Tupper is suddenly very angry and saying that any more cracks like that and he will be fetching me one.

I was not intending to make the joke, but do not have time to puzzle long over what I said. All over the vessel, the members are reeling in fish called codlings and pollacks and skates and some smaller gongher heels.

We are all being very happy and busy for two or three hours when suddenly the wind is increasing and the sea is becoming quite rough. The members, who had forgotten their indispositions, are suddenly turning green again, and Mr Skipper is shouting for lines inboard and we are going home.

When we are tying up in the calm water of the harbour, Mr Skipper is saying to be lining up for the share out. Two fish each.

Harry is saying two fish be booghered. He is promising the Sludgethorpe Darby and Joan Club a fish and chip supper, and what we are catching we are copping for.

'Sacks out, lads,' Harry is saying, and the members are producing sacks and filling them with fish from the boxes around the deck. Mr Skipper is now very angry and is trying unsuccessfully to snatch a sack from Harry.

Mr Harbottle is being very placatory and is giving Mr Skipper another sack which is lying nearby. Mr Skipper is plunging his hand into the sack to take out the fish, but is withdrawing it very quickly with a loud shout. It is the sack into which Harry put my gongher heel. By this time it is recovering from being hit with the iron bar and is biting most severely the hand of Mr Skipper.

Mr Skipper is saying, 'So you are thinking that is funny', picking up a codling (most fortunately dead) and with it hitting Mr Harbottle over the head, several times and most forcibly.

Harry is now giving Mr Skipper the promised punch up the throat, upon which he is falling down. This is giving the members enough time to pick up Mr Harbottle and leave the good ship *Venus*, taking with us enough of the fishes to make the Darby and Joan Club very grateful and to give us all some most enjoyable meals.

On the way back in the sharrybang, Mr Harbottle is waking up and being most angry with Harry. Harry is replying that the retention of fish caught by fair angling is the inalienable right of every freeborn Englishman, including Pakistanis, and to hell with what it is saying in the small print. Then he is saying, 'All together now', and we are singing:

> *We jolly sailor boys*
> *Are up and up aloft*
> *And the landlubbers lying down below, below, below,*
> *And the landlubbers lying down below.*

I am looking lovingly at my gongher heel and thinking that perhaps, after all, I have the sea in my blood.

Things that go burp in the night

This is your storyteller, the Man in Mucky Brown.

Night fishing can be an experience so eerie that even the hardest of men have been known to give up after a couple of sessions.

When Mad Mac came back from his last all-night angle his hair had turned completely white. He had tried to slosh a cow with a bag of groundbait and it had burst all over him. The groundbait, not the cow.

Seriously, though, the noises of night creatures can be highly unnerving. And to be *touched* by an unseen thing in the dark is the finest training in the world for the 200 metres.

But it's all in the mind. Once you know what the creatures are, the terror is gone. So this session of Uncle Clifford's Worry Corner is given over to an examination of the commoner night creatures and their identifiable characteristics.

A mouse walking over you can be recognised by its lightness, its little patty paws, and its habit of going, 'Eek, eek'.

A rat, though still light on its feet, is a bit heavier and not quite so cuddlesome. Once you have identified it, *you* go 'Eek, eek!'.

If a hedgehog walks over you as you squat on the bank, you get a pleasant tickling sensation and a free gift of fleas. If a hedgehog walks under you, you tend to rise a bit smartish.

A cow makes a noise like 'Moo', has big pointy feet and is very heavy. Cows which walk on people are not very popular.

A cold, clammy sensation creeping up your leg could mean that a snail has mistaken your superbly muscled calf for a stick of hairy rhubarb. Remove the snail before it gets too far up: it has a set of rasp-like teeth which can do naughties to the toughest of vegetables. There has so far been no recorded instance of a man-eating snail, but there's always a first time.

Sound magnifies at night, so even quite loud rustlings in the grass may be nothing more than mice, voles, rats or snails. Don't worry about the rapid thudding sound you can hear: that's your heart. Only worry when it stops.

Identification of sounds is very important. As we have heard, mice go, 'Eek, eek'. Cows go 'Moo', occasionally, 'Burrrp', and have a tendency towards heavy breathing. Owls 'owl. The big ones, that is. The Little Owl sounds like a flying tomcat, and this can be a bit disorientating.

Hedgehogs particularly make a lot of noise, grunting, snuffling and—when they back into each other—shouting, 'Gerroff!'

A nightjar goes, 'Urrrp!' and sounds quite revolting. A nightjar

which goes, 'Urrrp! Pardon', is one which has remembered its manners.

At dawn or dusk you may hear the cuckoo, with whose cry you are no doubt familiar. You may be puzzled by the occasional 'Oocuck'. This is a cuckoo flying backwards.

Elephants tread silently and you don't hear them until they are right on top of you. You will recognise an elephant on top of you by feeling first squashy and then dead. Take comfort from the fact that thanks to our temperate climate, elephants are very rare.

Ancient angling joke:

> *'Why are you sprinkling that powder along the bank?'*
> *'To keep the elephants away.'*
> *'But there aren't any elephants around here.'*
> *'Bloody good powder, isn't it?'*

I have known lads, beset by night-time noises, recite the old charm:

> *From ghoulies and ghosties,*
> *Long-leggity beasties*
> *And things that go bump in the night,*
> *May the Good Lord deliver us.*

But I don't recommend it. It fills your mind with all the spooks, weirds, haints, phantoms, ghouls, apparitions, zombies, vampires and monsters that otherwise you would never have thought of.

And it's no protection against the Big Fella, the monster that preys on lone anglers in the dark. Thirty feet high, and dirty green in colour. A pointed, hairless bonce with a single eye in the middle of the forehead. Short, thick legs with splayed, webbed feet. Powerful, seven-fingered hands which hang well below his knees. A beaky nose with wide nostrils to smell out his victims. A wide, slavering and fang-filled mouth with which he tears the victims to—

Hey, no. Come back. I was only kidding . . .

Uncle Clifford's Worry Corner

Not fair is it? Normal people can write to Claire Rayner or Marje Proops when things get a bit worriting. But anglers have nobody to whom they can pour out their little hearts. No warm, comforting bosom upon which they can lay their little pointy heads.

But fret no more. Parker has come to the rescue. Uncle Clifford's Worry Corner is now open for business. Pour out your little hearts, lads. But watch where you're putting your little pointy heads. Strangely, a lot of the queries come from women, wives and girl friends of anglers. You, darlings, may lay your head where'er you will.

* * *

Dear Uncle Clifford: Can you recommend a branch of angling which will cure the spots and pimples on my nose? *Unhappy Spotty-chops.*

Dear Unhappy Spottychops: Try reservoir fishing, facing the wind. In three weeks you'll have no skin left on your nose to have pimples on.

* * *

Dear Uncle Clifford: Every time my husband goes fishing, he comes back late, smelling of strong drink, beside himself with frustration and very violent. If his tea is not on the table, he beats me unmercifully. What shall I do? *Fearful Fanny, Farnworth.*

Dear Fearful Fanny: Make sure his tea's on the table.

* * *

Dear Uncle Clifford: My husband has started breeding worms for bait. He has built this revolting wormarium, full of foul compost and smelly tea leaves, which he says has to be sheltered from the weather. He has brought it indoors and insists on keeping it in the kitchen. I don't think this is right, do you? *Nauseated Nellie, Nuneaton.*

Dear Nauseated Nellie: No, I don't think it's right at all. The temperature in the kitchen fluctuates too much for the comfort of the worms and they don't like the smells. Move it into the bedroom.

* * *

Dear Uncle Clifford: My husband talks in his sleep, and the other night I heard him saying, 'What a beautiful little darling you are . . . take it steady now . . . watch what you're doing with those teeth . . . hey up—somebody's coming . . . ' What do you think it all means? *Suspicious Susan, Salford.*

Dear Suspicious Susan: Your husband is obviously reliving the playing of some particularly noteworthy fish. 'Beautiful little darling' is his reaction as it first breaks surface. 'Take it steady' as he turns its head away from a clump of reeds. 'Watch what you're doing with those teeth'—obviously he has caught a pike or a zander. 'Hey up—somebody's coming' means that in his dream he was fishing the water without a ticket and was fearful of the approach of a bailiff. I'd keep an eye on him if I were you.

*   *   *

Dear Uncle Clifford: My husband completely ignores me and spends every evening tying his flies. What can I do to win back his affections? *Thwarted, Thistlewaite.*

Dear Thwarted: Try untying his flies when he least expects it.

*   *   *

Dear Uncle Clifford: I am 23 years old and do not seem to have much success with the opposite sex, i.e. girls. My main hobby is fishing and I specialise in bream. I have other interesting hobbies such as maggot breeding and piscatorial taxidermy, that is to say, stuffing fish. I also have a very interesting job as production controller on a sewage farm.

I take a great pride in my personal appearance, having a bath every six weeks whether I need it or not, changing my pullover at the end of each season and my socks and underpants at least twice. Yet whenever I have approached any female girls, they have moved very swiftly in the opposite direction. What is wrong with me? *Lonely Leonard, Lincoln.*

Dear Lonely Leonard: It's the bream fishing that's wrong. It's not dashing enough, not exciting enough, for the girls of today. Try switching to pike. If that doesn't work, have a good scrub down with a yard brush.

*   *   *

Dear Uncle Clifford: I am 26 years old, blonde, 38–24–36 and a former Miss Tackle Box. My husband is a fanatical fisherman, going out every night and weekend. The only time I see him is at breakfast, and then he's usually got his head buried in *Angling Times.*

I'm only human, and I am beginning to feel the lack of normal companionship. In other words, I am burning with desire, loaded with lust, and on the verge of throwing myself at the first man who comes my way. What do you suggest? *Frantic, Frinton.*

Dear Frantic: Friday. Half past seven. Your place.

116

Please may I leave the towpath?

At the risk of offending the finer feelings of those who have never felt the need, I want to raise the burning topic: How Do You Do It On The Canal Bank?

Oh, it's all in the mind. Put down that pen, Disgusted of Didsbury, and read on a bit.

I'm talking about answering the Call of Nature. Having a tinkle. A Jimmy. A wee-wee.

There. I've said them. Some of the naughties.

The problem was brought home to me recently with some urgency, embarrassment and discomfiture. Caught short, I was, on an open stretch of bank. Not only was it open, but thronged with mums herding toddlers with tiddler nets, matronly ladies walking their little dogs and little husbands, and courting couples on the verge. The water itself was a-throng. With little lads in lifejackets doing the Duke of Edinburgh bit in kayaks, and blokes in yachting caps doing dashing things on pleasure boats.

Woe is me, I thought. I am undone. But I did not dare get anywhere near undone. There would be panic-stricken screams from affronted and affrighted womanhood. Freelance guardians of public decency would put down their binoculars and rush across the lock gates, macs flapping in the wind, to point the accusing finger. An official guardian of public decency, in big boots and a pointy hat, would flick over the pages of his notebook and moisten his pencil. Convinced he'd caught the Phantom Flasher of Lock 73 and seeing his sergeant's stripes already twinkling on his sleeve.

I was saved by a water vole. Who came paddling across the water, climbed on to a half-sunken piece of timber near the bank, woffled and scratched a bit, then dived off the near side.

To keep my mind off things, I went to have a look. And there, between the timber and the bank, was a little bay where the stonework had fallen in. What was more, a bay surrounded by tall nettles which screened the place from the towpath and arched over to hide it from the opposite bank as well.

Into the nettles I plunged. And into the bay did the necessary. Oh, the relief. The bliss. The sudden end to the long-drawn-out agony.

I'd forgotten about the vole. Poor little thing. He erupted at the surface of the bay, coughing and spluttering, scrabbled over the timber and crash-dived into the unsullied water beyond.

Sorry about that, little vole. Next time I see you I'll give you a butty.

To get back to the point. What *is* the answer?

I've known blokes carry windbreaks around with them on the balmiest of days for the very purpose of tinkling undetected. Known others carry a spare wellie. Others still who wore army surplus gas capes which reached down to the ground and gave plenty of room inside for the necessary manoeuvring.

Even then, with all the concealment, all the care not to offend the sensibilities of others, the Puritan streak in the British is so strong that people are upset by the fact that they *know* what you're doing, even if they can't *see* what you're doing.

It will be a long time before we treat the answering of Nature's calls in as adult a manner as the French. Dastardly Frenchmen think nothing of having a quick one in a waist-high whatnot on the boulevard and, with the free hand, raising the hat to a passing *demoiselle*. Dead civilised, that is.

Perhaps meantime we could use a special angler's cry. Something like 'Gardez l'eau!', which was shouted as a warning in the old days when people emptied slops from upper-storey windows into the street below.

We could try something like, 'Heads under!', 'Eyes down looking!' or 'Close 'em tight—here comes a fright!' But perhaps even that would not shield us from prying and unfriendly eyes. Like those of the old lady in the story who lived in the high rise flats near the canal. She called the police to complain that every day she could see nasty men relieving themselves on the towpath.

The police called round, looked through the window, and said, 'Sorry, missis. You can't even *see* the towpath from here.'

'Oh, yes you can,' she said. 'If you climb on top of the wardrobe and look through this telescope, you can see it perfectly . . . '

Does your liver come from Ireland?

Having already examined anglers' Injuries and Afflictions, the Parker Institute for the Study of Anglers' Nasties now turns its attention to ailments.

BRUMMAGEN BENDS

This is a form of influenza which unvaccinated anglers from other areas can come back with after fishing an away match in the Midlands. Brums who fish away from home can come back with Huddersfield Horrors, Salford Snookies, Westminster Wobblers or Cockney Cobblers.

LIFFEY LIVER

Along with Killarney Kidney, one of the ailments most prevalent among anglers who have just returned from an Irish fishing holiday. Visible symptoms are unfocused eyes, a highly coloured and pulsating nose, an unsteady gait and a tendency to burst into *Mother Machree* at the slightest provocation. Its causes are thought to be not entirely unconnected with some old Irish customs.

WADER'S WITHERS

If an anglers thighs are covered in damp silkweed which still harbours the attendant molluscs, crustaceans, fry and larvae, it is obvious that either:

> (a) His waders leak
> (b) His wellies are too short
> (c) He is too short
> (d) The river is too tall

The silkweed can be got rid of at the next match by letting the other anglers run their hooks through it to bait up. He need then be treated only for cuts, scratches and the restoration of any important bits hooked by mistake.

SWAMP FEVER, HAY FEVER, NETTLE RASH

Swamp Fever is contracted by staying too long in smelly ditches rooting for bloodworms. Early symptoms are a plastering of mud from head to toe and a horrible pong. The only cure is a scrape down and a 24-hour soak in sheep dip.

Hay Fever is contracted in high summer through spending too much time in the long grass. It is often a sign of a part-time sex maniac, especially if his keepnet and landing net show no signs of ever having been used.

Nettle rash. Anglers get this in some funny places, on account of there being no provision made by riparian owners for answering the calls of nature at the waterside. The angler should be wrapped in a dock leaf poultice and told to be more careful in the future.

SWINE FEVER, FOOT AND MOUTH, MYXOMATOSIS

Caused by getting too close to nature. There are no known cures for any of these conditions. He'll just have to be put down.

DEATH

This is a very serious ailment, from which few recover. It can be sudden, caused by:

1. Pulling the plug from a boat to let the water out.
2. Throwing an anchor over the side and forgetting to let go.
3. Saying 'Shoo' to an angry bull.
4. Trying to chicken out of paying for a round during post-match celebrations.
5. Forgetting to tell the Little Woman you might be late home after the match.

Or it can be lingering, caused by:

1. Fishing all day in the rain and slowly dissolving.
2. Allowing an advanced case of Basket Bum to degenerate into Duck's Disease, and discovering in the end that your legs are too little to carry you from the bank.
3. Lead poisoning, through trying to fix shot with your teeth during a bout of hiccups.
4. Alcohol poisoning, through over-compensation for lack of bites.

INSANITY

As anybody who takes up angling has to be potty to start with, this is not a condition to be taken too seriously. Any angler who's got it can take comfort from the fact that the others will never notice.

It's all in the stars

Got myself a book all about horoscopes. Tells you all about how the stars can influence your job, your love life, your fishing. Thought you might like to know how you're fixed anglingwise, Zodiacwise.

ARIES: March 21 to April 19

A leader, you are. A pioneer. Opening up new and uncharted waters and developing new angling techniques. Very energetic and highly versatile, you are. Too bloody good to be true, you are.

TAURUS: April 20 to May 20

You have a natural talent for all branches of planting and cultivating. You'll have to keep quiet about that if you want to get any fishing done. You are also good at breeding animals. I bet your gozzers are little bobby dazzlers.

You have a gift for singing. I would mention this to the lads on the bank the next time they're telling you to belt up.

GEMINI: May 21 to June 21

You have the gift of the gab or, to put it more politely, a flow of ready speech. You also have manual dexterity, combined with an analytical mind. I bet you make your own floats and tie your own flies.

With your talents you could be an inventor. If you didn't talk so much. And waste so much time making your own floats and tying your own flies.

CANCER: June 22 to July 22

Dead sensitive, you are. Can't bear to put a maggot on the hook. You could be an artist, an author, a poet, a doctor. So what are you doing working for the corporation, says the wife. Take no notice.

LEO: July 23 to August 23

You excel at decorating and interior design. It's blokes like you that spoil it for the rest of us.

You are also a dab hand in the kitchen. A superb cook.

How's your embroidery?

VIRGO: August 24 to September 23

You have an accountant's mind, and are very good at the exact and conservative use of money. You must be the bloke who cadges bait and never gets his hand down in the pub.

You would also make a very good preacher. You're not preaching to me before you've got a round in.

LIBRA: September 24 to October 23
You have grace and charm and are inclined to be beautiful. Gerroff.

SCORPIO: October 24 to November 22
Constantly searching, you are. Always on the trail. A manhunt fascinates you, so you would make a very good detective or traffic warden. Or a banzai bailiff, up the tree with your binoculars.

SAGITTARIUS: November 23 to December 21
Handsome, athletic, intelligent, wise, a superb fisherman with a great deal of charm and animal magnetism. Famous Sagittarians include Cliff Parker.

CAPRICORN: December 22 to January 19
You are the supreme specialist, able to take one small sphere of endeavour and develop it to perfection. Like fishing for gudgeon all your life.

A very materialistic character you are, able to make a place for yourself in the business world. Probably flogging gudgeon.

AQUARIUS: January 20 to February 18
You're not doing so badly. Wonderful intellectual equipment, you have. Ideal professor material. Not hidebound, either, but always investigating progressive ideas. You can organise and reform. And write like a dream. Mind if we swop places?

PISCES: February 19 to March 20
You live in a world of illusion and favour pantomime or eccentric dancing. As befits the sign of the fish, you are interested in liquids and often make the trade in liquids your life's work or study. Mad Mac is a Piscean. I should have known.

... being extracts from the diaries and other documents of the Sludgethorpe Waltonians. This from the diary of Edward (Big Eddie) Fanshawe, licensee of *The Bricklayer's Arms*.

Big Eddie's life sentence

Whenever anyone says how nice it must be to keep a pub, I ask them to come around when the fishing mob are in. They're enough to put anybody off for good.

I'm trying to build up a good class of trade, and I've tried everything to keep that lot out of here. And what's happened? I've finished up as an Honorary Life Member of the Sludgethorpe Waltonians.

I should never have sent them that set of darts and the sarky note about it stopping them bending the points on the pub arrows. That daft old devil Harbottle, the Waltonians' chairman, took the note literally. The next thing I know, they've all trooped in here, presented me with a Life Membership Certificate and a stuffed pike, and stood around waiting for drinks on the house.

That pike. Looks as if they've played football with it. Scales missing, tail frayed, nose cracked, colour gone to a dirty brown. I've had to put it up over the bar, haven't I? And now the place looks like a licensed fishmonger's.

When I think of the trouble that lot have caused in the past. There was Harry Turner—and he's been a troublemaker since he was a lad—assaulting my wife with a dead duck because she clouted his ferret. He was only letting that revolting little animal eat the cheese nibbles off the counter, that's all.

Then we had Albert Rowbottom—God rest his soul, the silly old duffer—putting that dart right through Cyril Higginson's nose. I wouldn't have cared, but Cyril was sitting six feet away from the dartboard. When he'd had a few, Old Rowbottom couldn't even *see* the board, let alone hit it.

Oh, yes, and there was that business of Jim Kerrigan's home brew. Gallons of it, he made. Then he invited all his Waltonian mates to his house, got them stewed as newts, and then brought them all round here to top up.

If I'd known they were in that state, they'd have been straight out. But the three who could still walk got the pints in for the rest of them. At closing time the place was littered with bodies. The three who could still walk carried out old Rowbottom, then they collapsed on top of him. I had to lug all the rest of them out on to the pavement and get Joe Hayes to bring his lorry round and help me cart them home.

And who was in trouble next day? *Me*. For propping them up against their front doors and leaving them to be massacred by their wives.

It's better during the close season. At least they come in in twos and threes, wearing some sort of civilised getup. But during the season, when the whole mob has arrived in their fishing clobber after a match . . . phew!

They look like a bunch of Castro's chuck-outs for a start. Camouflage jackets, bush hats, ammunition boots . . . I keep telling them, 'You'll find Che Guevara in the Public Bar, you lot.' But they've never been known to take a hint.

Once they've been in for an hour, and the place has warmed up, then it starts. The pong. Until you've smelt 25 anglers drying off in a confined space, you've smelt nothing. It's a wonder the plastic ivy doesn't wilt.

Had a lovely couple in a few months back. Came in an Aston Martin. Distinguished looking middle-aged gent and a very attractive blonde young lady. His niece, I should have thought. They sat quietly in one corner and were no trouble at all. Very good class of customer altogether. Gave the place a bit of tone.

Then Harry Turner comes in with Horace Harris and that little Paki bloke from the plastics factory. First thing he says, addressing the young lady, is, 'Hello, love. Not seen you around for a bit. Have you left the biscuit factory, then? Bet they miss you in the packing department.'

That was it. The couple just swept out, got into the Aston Martin and drove off.

'She was never the same, that one,' said Turner, 'after they put her on round boxes.'

I should never have sent those darts.

Treat 'em rough

I've been reading in the paper about how women like to be dominated.

The bigger the villain, apparently, the more they love him. They like to be ruled, crushed, kept under and knocked about a bit. The dream of even the most respectable woman, it says here, is of one day meeting The Brute who will do naughty things to her.

It figures, when you think of some of the blokes women have falled for. Rasputin, Casanova, Napoleon, Heathcliff, Byron, King Kong, Mad Mac and Big McGinty.

So perhaps we nice lads are playing it all wrong. Perhaps by being so good, kind, considerate and helpful, we are not only spoiling our fishing, but losing the respect of our wives as well.

Ever ready in the cause of science and marital harmony, I think I have the answer: The Parker Nine-Point Plan for Dominance of Women, All-Round Villainy and Trouble-Free Fishing.

1. If you want to go fishing, go. No matter what wants doing around the house. Tell her to cut the flaming grass herself.

2. If you want to keep maggots in the fridge, keep 'em in the fridge. And if you want to breed them in the coal shed—or in the front room for that matter—you just go right ahead.

3. If you want to liquidise worms in the Kenwood Chef, liquidise 'em. And let the missis clean up after you.

4. If you want to use her best set of nonstick saucepans for boiling your wheat, hemp, tares or pith, use 'em. Leave 'em in the sink afterwards.

5. If you want to stay out all night fishing, or whatever else takes your fancy, you just stay out. All weekend if you like.

6. If you want to celebrate with the lads after the match, celebrate. Properly. Get stoned, squiffed, stonkers. Or palatic, as they say in my country. Pissed, as they say in impolite society. As a lord. As a ferret. As a newt. As a fiddler's bitch.

7. When you get home, if you want to dump your tackle, clobber and damp nets in a trail from the back yard, through the living-room and up the stairs, dump 'em.

8. If at any time on your return home, the meal is either burnt or not ready, and the Little Woman is doing her pieces, give her one. They love it. It says here.

If that doesn't work, give her another. She'll be your slave for life.

If her mother's there, looking daggers, give her one, too. For luck.

9. Let me know how you get on. If enough of you survive, I might try it myself.

Hole in the toad

Proud of myself, I was. About to become a daddy again. About a thousand of them this time.

Tadpoles.

(What did you think I meant? Irresistible I may be, but there are limits.)

No, I'd topped up the world-renowned Parker ponds with frog spawn. Making sure that the little fellers would have a trouble-free childhood. Ready with the tins of vitamin-enriched Kattyponks to bring them up as well-nourished tadders from the moment they entered this hostile world. Steeling myself against the heartbreak of the time when, with little legs akimbo, they would hop off and leave me.

Then I read in the paper about the toads getting flattened as they crossed the road to their spawning grounds. Hundreds of them finishing up as toad macadam under the wheels of unfeeling juggernauts.

This, I decided, was a job for Battyman. And Robin.

I rang up Mad Mac.

'Buddy mate,' I said, in tones of breathless urgency, but steely and determined with it, 'we must make the world safe for toads.'

'Strange you should mention that,' he said.

'Why?' I queried. 'By some miracle of extra sensory perception, were you thinking exactly the same thing?'

'No,' said Mac. 'It's just strange that you should mention it. What the bloody hell are you on about?'

'There is no time to waste,' I replied. 'Not a moment to lose.'

'No,' said Mac. 'See you in the *Cock and Bottle*.'

'In about ten minutes,' said I, urgently. 'Roger and . . . er . . . Roger and er . . . '

'Out?'

'Out.'

*   *   *

Pausing in the *Cock and Bottle* for only two hours to discuss the plan of campaign, Mac and I left for the Killing Grounds.

The afternoon sun was high in the sky, and on the shimmering tarmac of the A41 was nary a toad to be seen. Only lots of cars and bloody great lorries exceeding the speed limit. The drivers of which hooted us and made rude gestures every time we stepped off the verge with our plastic bags.

'I have an idea,' said Mac, as the wheels of the fiftieth lorry did nasties to his toecap. 'Let's go home.'

'Mac, old friend,' said I, sternly, 'I'd always thought better of you. We cannot—nay, *must* not —desert these defenceless little toads in their hour of need. We shall trek through the uncharted wastes across the road, find their pond, and rescue them.'

'But if they are already in the pond,' said Mac, 'they don't need rescuing.'

'Who,' I asked, fixing him with a withering gaze, 'is in charge of this expedition?'

*   *   *

To cut a short story long, there were these teenage toads. Looking at each other in about 18 inches of gunjy old water. And, being adolescent and shy, not knowing quite what to do about it.

Quick as a flash I was off with my boots and socks and had my immaculately pressed trousers rolled above the knee.

'Har har,' laughed Mac. 'Huckleberry Fink.'

'Huckleberry,' I snarled, 'Schmuckleberry.'

'Make sure they're toads,' shouted Mac from the top of the bank.

'I didn't spend the best years of my irrecoverable youth studying Natural History for nothing,' I replied. 'Toads are the ones with warts and little legs like you. Har har har.'

'That's right, buddy. And frogs are the slimy ones with big bellies like you. Har har har.'

I did not think that was very funny.

Anyway, I grabbed four toads in ninety seconds. Which does not say much for their powers of survival. If I had been a nasty-minded pike, I could have cleaned up the whole pond in ten minutes.

*   *   *

Back at the ranch house, we turned out the toads and dropped them carefully into the frog ponds.

The last one out of the bag looked a bit funny.

'I hate to mention it,' said Mac. 'You being the expert and that. But that toad is a frog.'

'Never,' I said. 'It's a bit slimy, but it's only got little—bloody 'ell . . . '

It *was* a frog. A one-legged frog. With only one back leg, that is, and a stump. When I caught it I must have been looking at the wrong side.

'Never mind, darlin',' said Mac as he put it gently into the pond. 'You can be mother . . . '

Doctor Dumdum's Electric Wonder Oil

I used to say that Mad Mac was born out of his time and had missed his true vocation.

With his gift of the gab and lack of principle, he should have been on a medicine wagon in the old Wild West. Selling snake oil. Guaranteed to cure all ills, mend broken legs and bring the dead back to life. At only a dollar a bottle.

I should never have said it.

We were having a conference on the relative architectural merits of old English country inns. I was poorly, sickening for a bout of 'flu and talkig dowd by doze.

'Your troubles are over, buddy mate,' said Mac. 'I so happen to have with me a bottle of Doctor Dumdum's Electric Wonder Oil which I bought from a little Indian with a turban in a pub. And with which I have already effected several miraculous cures. Take this home, rub it in where it hurts, and your pain will be no more.'

In the past I have almost died from Mac's nature cures, but this time I was past caring. By nightfall it was hurting everywhere, so I rubbed the oil all over, fell into bed and passed straightaway into a sleep that might well have been my last.

Next morning I awoke, convinced that the oil had fulfilled all Mac's promises. I sprang out of bed, opened the window, took a deep breath and collapsed in a massive coughing fit. I dragged my pain-racked body back to the bed. 'You're not coming back in here,' said Dearly Beloved. 'You smell like a box of old kippers.'

I did, too. With my nose bunged up, I couldn't smell a thing. But the whole family kept to windward until I'd had a shower. All except the cat, who bit a chunk out of my leg.

Seal oil it was, according to the label. Mixed with sulphuric acid, turps and one or two other yuckies. Mac said Eskimos swear by it. Why they're not extinct I'll never know.

A week later I met Mac again. And I was still talking dike dat. Dowd by doze.

'Hello, buddy mate,' he said. 'My, my, you're looking well. Doctor Dumdum's did the trick, eh?'

'Doe,' I said. 'Id bluddy well diddud. I got banned frob de barital couch, shunned by de kids ad attacked by de cat. Ad I'b still poorly.'

'Ah,' said Mac. 'What you need is another bottle. I've got half a dozen still left on account of the little Indian feller in the turban gave me discount for quantity.'

'You cad take dat half dudden,' I said, 'ad stick dem ub your doze. Wod by wod. Sideways.'

'Some people,' said Mac, all peeved, 'have no gratitude. But do not worry, faithless old friend. I have another use for it. I'm going to dip my baits in it. There is not a fish in this world which can resist Doctor Dumdum's Electric Wonder Oil. You just wait and see.'

I waited. But I never saw. Every time I have met Mac since, he has been full of his success with Doctor Dumdum's. How the fish were snatching the oil-soaked bait on the drop at every cast. How tiring it was to have to empty the keepnet so often. How upset he was at giving all the other lads on the bank a complex. How, shortly, he would have to overcome his natural modesty and enter some of his weights for *Angling Times* Catch of the Year awards.

Funny. Those mammoth catches have always happened when I've not been there. When Mac's been fishing with me, he's always left the Wonder Oil at home.

'I took you at your word, old buddy,' he said. 'That you did not wish to know about the oil. And I could not embarrass you by fishing with it alongside. I have my sensitivities even if some people do not.'

I have the nasty theory that Mac may be bending the old veracity a bit. That he is telling whopping great fibs just to get his own back.

But I have another, nicer, theory that he may just be telling the truth. He has been known to do it once or twice. And I feel I may be missing out.

I cannot humiliate myself by begging forgiveness and the loan of a bottle of Wonder Oil. That's why I'm combing the pubs. Incognito. Wearing the false wig and ginger beard. Looking for a little Indian. In a turban. Giving discount for quantity.

The last of the ogres

Angling is no occupation for the hypersensitive.

I discovered this the first time I went fishing with Mad Mac.

He wouldn't put the bait on because of his religion. Squeamishness. Mac is a confirmed Squeam.

He wouldn't even look as I sorted through the maggots to find him one with character. And turned a horrible green when I switched to worms.

In spite of everything, he caught a couple of roach. I had to unhook them while he looked the other way.

After a couple of hours he said, 'I'm hungry.'

'Have a butty,' I said, taking my hand from the maggot tin. diving into the basket and holding out a beautiful liver sausage and tomato job.

'Thanks,' he said. And then noticed my hand, covered in fish and worm slime, speckled with scales and empty maggot skins.

He was sick all over my welly.

Then there was the time, fishing with Number One Son, when I felt peckish.

'Where's the grub, me old fruit?'

'I didn't bring any.'

'Great. What am I supposed to do? Starve to death?'

'I did bring some bread and cheese for bait. They're both fresh.'

'That'll do. Where is it?'

'In that old maggot tin.'

I opened the tin, took out the cheese and chomped heartily. There was something strange about the flavour, a bit high for cheddar. Something strange, too, about the texture, which felt suspiciously like sawdust.

'Son of mine, did you . . . er . . . wash out the maggot tin after we got back last week?'

'Well, actually. Since you ask. In a manner of speaking. What I mean is. Er, sort of. But perhaps . . . '

'Did you or didn't you?'

'No.'

Exit papa, Stage Left, making noises like 'Yuk!', 'Bleah!' and 'Aaaaaaaaaaargh!'

Let's face it. Some of the things we take for granted as a normal part of angling are pretty revolting.

Handling maggots. Used as we are to them as bait, it's always a shock to come across them in their wild state when we pick up a dead bird or mouse. That horrible, slimy, heaving mass, straight out of a Hammer film—surely they can't be the cousins of the little beauties we play with so tenderly every weekend?

And as for the old match anglers who kept maggies warm under their tongues in cold weather—how did they do it, Stanley?

No wonder we get black looks in the pub when we've spent an hour poking around reeking ditches for bloodworms, turning over cowpats in the hope of finding something tempting underneath, or spiking on lengths of smelly fishguts and nauseous squid.

But hold on. Hang about. Wait a minute.

Perhaps it is not we who are revolting after all. Perhaps everybody else is too refined. We do, after all, live in an age dedicated to removing all traces of our animality.

We spray ourselves all over with stuff to take away our cosy human smell. (When I say *we*, I don't mean us, of course. I mean *them*.) We powder ourselves from top to bottom, and further down than that. We shave our armpits. We are scared of using a toothpaste that doesn't promise a tingling fresh ring of thing in the close-up zone. We take tablets to rid our breath of unpleasant things like the smell of scotch. Our socks are treated with chemicals that leave our old plates smelling like violets. After every shave we slap on stuff that makes us smell like the Queen of the Fairies. And I do mean fairies.

Our food is bought ready scrubbed, peeled, homogenised, shrink-wrapped and unrecognisable. Even the flavour has been removed so that we don't actually taste anything resembling something that once grew in the earth or walked about on it. How many hausfraus nowadays buy a chicken with its feathers on and its guts still inside, or buy a bunny with its coat on?

Our beer has been rationalised out of all recognition. Of *course* it never goes off; there's nothing in the plastic gnat's hiss that *can* go off.

So perhaps the angler now stands for something more than just the quiet waterside philosopher. Perhaps, in staying close to the earth, in keeping contact with the creatures which swim, walk, fly, or crawl over it, we are preserving something for future generations: the ability to operate as a human animal and not as a deodorised, computerised, compliant zombie.

Perhaps we are the last of the ogres in the land of the pygmies. (If you haven't read the poem *Ogres and Pygmies*, by Robert Graves, I strongly recommend it. End of Culture for the Masses bit.)

And perhaps we ought not to give up our ogrehood without a fight. There are very few of us left with this gift—this very precious gift—of being so thoroughly, unutterably, unashamedly and irretrievably . . . revolting.

. . . being extracts from the diaries and other documents of the Sludgethorpe Waltonians. This from the diary of the former Miss Dimity Docherty, now the wife of Mr Sidney Puddephatt, one of the Waltonians' up-and-coming matchmen.

My mother never told me

My dad said he wouldn't hear of it, me having a mixed marriage.

He belongs to the Slagville Piscatorials, and the thought of me marrying a Sludgethorpe Waltonian was just too much for him. He said that such a thing had never happened before in the history of the club and that he dreaded to think what the committee would feel about it.

What was wrong with his own lads, the Piscatorials? he kept asking. I said that if he had four hours to spare, I could tell him. Bunch of roughnecks. At least my Sidney always wears a clean collar to work.

He stamped off to the pub, going on about the shame of it all. Just before he slammed the door, he shouted to my mother that he was having no lass of his marrying out, and that was the end of it.

It wasn't the end of it, though. 'Leave it to me,' said mam, and she was waiting for him when he got back. With the coal shovel. Next day we put the banns up.

It was a pity the wedding was on a Saturday, because both clubs had a match that morning. The ceremony wasn't until three o'clock, but even then half the male guests turned up wearing wellingtons under their trousers.

Sidney looked ever so overcome when I arrived at the altar. He was deathly pale and having a real struggle to fight back the tears.

'Don't worry, dear heart,' I whispered to him. 'Every bridegroom feels nervous on his wedding day.'

'It's not that,' he said with a catch in his voice. 'We lost.'

The ceremony went without a hitch, thank goodness. But when we got outside the church, there were members from both clubs forming a guard of honour with crossed rods, rod rests and landing nets.

Two of the guard of honour produced placards, one saying *Nice One, Sidney*, and the other saying *May Your Troubles Only Be Tiddlers.*

I suppose they meant well, but it really spoiled the wedding photographs.

There was a brief scuffle when one of the Slagville men, who was standing opposite Chalky White, the Sludgethorpe champion matchman, had a sort of nervous spasm which resulted in the net he was holding being jammed right over Mr White's head.

Oh, and the dreadful jokes in the speeches at the reception. 'If Sidney had only kept his mouth shut, he'd never have been hooked.' 'I don't know what Sidney used for bait, but if he could bottle it he'd make a fortune.' And, of course, a dozen variations on, 'She was only a fisherman's daughter.'

There was worse to come later in the evening. Mr Harbottle, the Waltonians' chairman, insisted on making a speech about a marriage of true minds, a union which would heal the long-standing breach between the clubs. Perhaps in the not-too-distant future, he said, we could look forward to a merger between Sludgethorpe and Slagville, the two associations which for generations had been the envy of the angling world.

I suppose it was my dad's fault, really, because he stood up and shouted, 'Over my dead body!' My mam said that could easily be arranged and hit him with an electric toaster.

Chalky White leapt to his feet and shouted, 'No federation without consultation!' He was dragged down by Harry Turner, who told him to save that for the shop stewards' meeting on Monday. By this time, however, some of the Slagville men were on their feet and chanting: 'Sludgethorpe out! Sludgethorpe out!'

I don't know who threw it, but a cream bun came sailing over and hit Mr Harbottle straight between the eyes.

My mam said that it was time for Sidney and me to be on our way, and that if we got outside, the car would be waiting. We tried to say goodbye to people, but there were a lot of chairs being pushed back and scuffles breaking out all over the room. Sidney and I could not even say goodbye to our fathers because they were rolling about under the table and pummelling each other.

My mam and Sidney's mam pushed a way out for us and bundled us into the car. The driver was very surprised at the amount of noise going on inside, but mam said they were playing forfeits. When a wellington boot came flying through a window in a shower of glass, he said it was a bloody funny way to play forfeits, but he drove off and we were in plenty of time for the train.

Ever since I was little I have been told that her wedding night is the most magical, glorious experience of a woman's life. If that's so, I just daren't think what the rest of my life has in store for me.

First there was the dead pike wrapped in my nightie, with a note saying, 'Watch his teeth, love'. And a squirming mass of maggots in my cold-cream jar.

Finally I climbed into bed next to my beloved Sidney and put my arms around him. He was wearing a brooding expression and trembling slightly.

'Sidney,' I whispered.

He did not reply.

'Sidney, darling,' I whispered.

Not a word.

'What are you thinking about, my pet?' I asked.

He gave a deep, shuddering sigh. Then spoke.

'Do you know, if I'd been a bit quicker on the strike with that flaming bream, we might have been in with a chance.'

My mother should have told me.

Potty time

Anglers keep coming to me for professional advice. And rightly so. Me being the founder and head of the Parker Institute for the Study of Anglers' Nasties.

The Psychiatric Branch is doing the business at the moment.

'Cliffers,' they say. 'We can talk to you because we know you're potty.'

'Have a care,' I say. 'You think *I'm* potty. You should meet my brother.'

The preliminaries over, they pour out their little hearts. A couple of hours later, only the price of a few pints lighter, they go on their way rejoicing. Because they've realised there's nowt wrong with them. At least, nothing that another angler would notice.

They always assume that their fears, their phobias, their complexes, are based on fantasy. Which is the thing which scares them most. Once they accept that they're all based on fact, they haven't a care in the world.

So to cut down the queue at the back door of the *Queen and Cobbler*, I shall run through the questions asked most frequently:

Q: I am an angler. Am I therefore, and by definition, mad?

A: Yes. Now forget it.

Q: I feel I am suffering from a Rejection Complex. Am I?

A: No. You are just rejected. You are scruffy, unshaven, smelly, keep unsocial hours and are often under the influence of Demon Drink. Therefore people avoid you, turn their backs, look down their noses, turn you off buses and throw you out of pubs. What else do you expect?

Q: I have a Persecution Complex. People seem to be spying on me all the time, invading my privacy, tracing my movements, logging my comings and goings. Can this be so?

A: Yes. If the Almighty had not meant us to feel persecuted, He would not have made people like bailiffs, club secretaries, policemen, traffic wardens, wives, mothers-in-law and neighbours. You just cannot go around fishing waters without a ticket, climbing reservoir fences at three in the morning, leaving your car for twelve hours on a double yellow line and coming back singing *Delilah* at the top of your voice without one, some or all of these people taking an interest. Not to mention the Truant Officer from the factory Personnel Department.

Q: I have irrational fears. That sooner or later I will be bitten by horses, trodden on by cows, butted by bullocks, nipped by crayfish, stung by nettles,

*torn by barbed wire, ruptured by a deceptively high stile and finish up by
falling into swift, deep and icy water. Could these things ever happen to me?*

A: Yes. Just give them time.

*Q: I have a fear of little creatures, like spiders, earwigs, voles, mice,
rats and hedgehogs. I dream of them crawling all over me as I fish during
the day, and creeping into my sleeping bag when I'm night fishing. What can
I do to cure these nightmares?*

A: What nightmares? The only thing you won't get crawling
over you on the bank during the day is Miss World. Before you go
to sleep, try to imagine Brigitte Bardot crawling into your sleeping
bag. Meanwhile, think kindly of hedgehogs.

*Q: I get claustrophobia in pubs after a fishing match. After a certain
length of time, I have to dash outside. What is the cause of this?*

A: Either you're caught short or it's your turn to pay.

*Q: My wife is joining a Fishing Widows' Club. I'd like to know (a)
Why? and (b) What do these women get up to?*

A: (a) If you don't know now, you never will. (b) There are some
things it is better not to know.

Danglimetrics

Once upon a time, when the world was very young and people had money to spend on such rubbish, I wrote a book called *Lazometrics*, which was a programme of exercises for lazy men. The exercises cost you no physical effort at all. Neither did they do you any good.

(I wrote a sequel called *Sexometrics*, which was sex for lazy men, but the publisher decided against it on the grounds of public order and decency.)

I mention all this dreary stuff merely to establish my qualifications as the author of Danglimetrics, a system of exercises for dozy anglers.

Exercises for energetic, athletic anglers are easy enough. You do all the hairy stuff that the PTIs shouted at you to do in the mob. Fifty press-ups. Twenty times round the square in full pack. Running on the spot for an hour because he'd gone into the NAAFI for a quick lunge at the bird on the tea urn and forgotten all about you.

But exercises for dozy anglers are much more subtle, much more refined. Steeped in aesthetic and spiritual qualities rather than sweat and embrocation. So follow me, you delicate little lotus blossoms, to Danglimetrics.

The three basic Danglimetric routines have a social and educational value, as well as preparing the angler for the day's activities: They are:

1. Wife Waking
2. Cat Throwing and Weather Forecasting
3. Elbow Flexing

Wife Waking

Essential for an early start, ensuring that the angler goes out into the chill of the morning warmly wrapped and well nourished. It also enables the wives to start their housework much earlier, a consideration they greatly appreciate.

1. Open one eye and focus on the ceiling. By the pattern of the cracks you will establish that you are, in fact, at home.

2. With gentle flexing movements of the wrist and fingers, establish the position of the good lady's bum.

3. Place the sole of one foot (or of both feet if she is of noble proportions) against one or both cheeks.

4. Heave. Until you hear the crash on the floor. Accompany the heave with the Dangli Sutra chant of, '*Lessavacupatee . . . lessavacupatee . . .*'

Cat Throwing and Weather Forecasting

This fascinating exercise combines meteorology with exercise for both yourself and your pussycat, gets the circulation going and ensures that before you leave the house you know what you're in for.

1. With the left hand, grasp the front door handle. With the right, grasp the scruff of the cat's neck. (Or the tail or back leg if it's being unco-operative.)

2. Open the door smartly. At the same time swing the cat in a graceful arc, letting go at the end of the swing.

3. Close the door smartly before the cat can get back in.

Now observe the effects of the conditions outside. A well-thrown pussycat is much more reliable than a piece of seaweed. For example:

A cat which turns soggy indicates rain.

A cat which goes stiff all over indicates hard frost.

A cat which disappears suddenly sideways, with no apparent movement of the limbs, indicates a fresh to gale force wind.

A cat which disappears suddenly downwards indicates the presence of snowdrifts or floodwater. (You can tell the difference by the bubbles.)

Elbow Flexing

This exercise keeps the right elbow so supple that never again will you muff a cast through lack of flex. Or flex a cast through lack of muff.

The smooth action it imparts is also a very useful social asset. You will hear the girls whispering, 'Who is that man with the super-smooth action over there? Yes, that gorgeous creature with the red nose and pot belly.'

For this exercise you need only the simplest of equipment: a counter or other raised flat surface, just below elbow height, a pint pot and the wherewithal to keep it filled.

1. Raise the right forearm to elbow height, parallel with the floor.

2. In one smooth movement, still keeping the arm parallel with the floor, swing the forearm round to grasp the handle of the pint pot.

3. Bending the arm smoothly at the elbow, raise the pot to the lips and take a gentle sip. Before or after, depending on the degree of flex or thirst, give the Dangli Sutra greeting of, 'Here is mud in your thingy, O snatcher of tiddlies. And may your wellies never grow wobbly.'

This is the most popular of all Danglimetric exercises, practised by those anglers who really care about their flexing. One of these days some of them might actually get down to the water.

A happy Hallowe'en to all our readers

Hallowe'en is the time when the witches, warlocks and fairies roam abroad. When the spirits of the dead return to their homes. When all the powers of darkness—eh, shurrup. I'm frightening myself silly.

What I wanted to bring to your attention was the number of old Celtic rituals and ceremonies, particularly those of Hallowe'en which are still observed by anglers today. Ceremonies such as:

Placating the Water Spirit

The druids would sit along the banks of a river and, at regular intervals, would cast upon the water offerings of bread and cheese. Occasionally they would exchange ritual chants:

> *Anything-doing-your-end-Dai-bach?*
> *Not-a-flaming-nibble-boyo.*

If the Water Spirit was pleased with their offerings, it would reward them with miraculous draughts of fish. If it were not pleased, there would be no fish, the sky would darken and the druids would get rained on solidly for eight hours.

At the end of such a day, the druids would go back to the sacred grove and knock off a few human sacrifices. Today we just go home and kick the cat.

The Clouting of the Puca

The Puca was a mischievous little spirit who ran around at Hallowe'en getting up ancient Celtic noses with his merry pranks, such as poisoning the fruit and turning the beer flat.

He still appears today at the river bank in the form of a snotty-nosed, crop-headed delinquent who heaves bricks at floats, drops old railway sleepers from bridges on to unsuspecting anglers and nicks any bits of tackle not tied down.

The old Celtic charm for banishing the Puca was to chant under one's breath, 'Stay where you are, you little Puca, you, and see what Nunky's got.' Creeping upon him stealthily the while as he was engrossed in demolishing a piece of bridgework.

When one had moved close enough, one drew back one's right arm. And then brought it swiftly forward to make symbolic and painful contact with the nitty little pointy head.

One then had to move away in case the Puca returned with his

father, who almost always turned out to be a bigger Puca than he was.

Washing Away the Sorrows

When the old Celtic fishermen returned empty handed, they assembled in a sacred hut called the *bhu-zar*. There they were served with fiery potions whose hallucinatory effects banished their sorrows and lifted their spirits.

Before long the hut would be ringing with lusty Celtic songs— *She's A Lassie From Penmaenmawr, My Girl's A Blaenau Ffestiniog Girl,* and *I Belong To Llanfairpwllgwyngyllgogerychwyndrobwllllantysiliogogogoch.*

Just as the merrymaking was at its height, however, a bell would ring. Striking fear into the heart of every man there. And the genial host who had been serving the potions would tear away his smiling mask to reveal the hate-filled face of a warlock. Casting a baleful eye over the hushed assembly, he would utter the following spell in tones of dread and menace:

Let's-have-your-glasses-now-gents-please . . . well-past-TIME!

And the whole company would rush screaming and gibbering into the inhospitable night.

Crushing the Rhadiowon

The Rhadiowon was a spirit who was imprisoned in a little metal casket and who tormented everyone within earshot with shrieks and wails. The casket was carried around by an evil geni who delighted in the noise, and who refused all appeals to take it somewhere else.

At Hallowe'en, a passing knight crushed the casket with his iron-shod heel, releasing the spirit and bringing peace and quiet once more to the countryside.

This drama is often re-enacted today on the river bank by anglers with sensitive ears, and followed by the ritual words, 'Sorry, mate—was that your transistor?'

The Spurning of the Swan Woman

One day a fisherman returned home unexpectedly and caught his wife passing the time of day with the charcoal burner, the ancient Celtic equivalent of the coalman.

As a punishment she was turned into a swan, and doomed to stay in that form until her husband forgave her. Every year at Hallowe'en she returned to beg forgiveness, and every year he drove her from his door with blows and imprecations.

How often today do we see anglers still driving away swans with blows and naughty words. It's just as well. Anybody who relents and says nice things to a swan might find himself with a beautiful young woman on his hands.

And how do you explain *that* to the wife?

For ladies only

Gather round, girls. Draw the curtains and lock the door. This is for your eyes only. The Parker Seven-Point Plan for Restoring Marital Harmony and Bringing Back a Gleam into the Old Man's Eye.

Does your husband pay you scant attention lately? Has he lost the gallantry of his courting days? Instead of bringing you a 3 lb. box of chocolates done up in a blue ribbon with a pussycat in full colour on the lid, does he sling over two ounces of misshapes in a brown paper bag?

Is his angling coming between you? Does he spend more time with his pinkies than he does with you? Or, perish the thought, do you suspect him of doing something other than angling? Some naughty thing that will eventually get him into the *News of the World*? *Sex Crazed Angler and Blonde Barmaid in Love Nest Drama*, that kind of thing?

Or do you just wish he were less of a slob? That he'd shave now and again? Cut his toenails? Or take his wellies off before he gets into bed?

Girls, your troubles are over. Uncle Clifford has done it again. Put the Master Plan into practice and within three short weeks life will have taken on a new meaning. New horizons will have opened up. Glowing vistas. Hitherto undreamed of dimensions. And all that.

1. *Start as you mean to carry on*. With love. Four times a day, close your eyes, take a deep breath and say to yourself ten times over, 'I *love* that little feller'. It may be a bit of a strain at first, but persevere. Before you know it, you'll have talked yourself into it.

2. *Reject all evil thoughts*. Think nothing but good of the lad. If he's out a bit later than he should be, or you think he should be (there *is* a subtle difference) do not conjure up visions of sin and debauchery.

He is relaxing with his trusty comrades after a backbreaking and soul-destroying week's toil in the Concrete Jungle. Which he undertook purely for the sake of you and the little ones.

A nobler, finer, more unselfish being never walked the face of the earth. Wonder if they *will* ever make him a saint?

3. *Take an interest in his hobby*. Angling, that is. Learn to tell a pinkie from a gozzer. Offer to take the bend from his rod rest and clean the weed from his swingtip.

4. *Sympathise*. When he comes back wheezing and soggy after falling in the cut, breaking his rod and dropping his butties in the water, don't dismiss it with a curt, 'Serves you right . . . a grown man like you messing about like a little lad . . .'

No. Take off his wet things, towel him down, wrap him in a warm dressing-gown, sit him in front of the fire, give him a big hot meal, a cigar and a large glass of the hard stuff. As he is tucking into the Lobster Thermidor, slip into something more comfortable. Nestle at his feet in the firelight, all cleavage and mascara, and say, 'Now darling, tell me all about it. Or is there anything else I can do to take your mind off it . . . ?'

(If he says, 'Yes, you can get me the tomato sauce,' control yourself. These things take time.)

5. *Nourish him.* An active sport like angling burns up the calories which must be replaced if he is to function properly as the bread-winner and master of the household.

Get up with him before he goes fishing, however early it may be, and rustle him up a decent breakfast. Nothing elaborate. Oyster soup, salmon mousse, roast ptarmigan, coq au vin, scotch fillet steak poached in malt whisky, boar's head with apple sauce, stuffed peacock, Tibetan goat cheese and peaches in hot brandy sauce ought to be enough to keep out the chill for a while.

Just to make sure, fill his favourite pint mug to two-thirds of its depth with hot, strong tea, and the remaining third with rum.

If he falls down the front steps after that lot, remember not to upbraid him. Pick him up, dust him down, and point him in the direction of the bus stop.

6. *Warm and relax him.* When he comes in from a windy, rainy, stressful day by the bank.

The best way of doing this is by the oral administration of some spirituous liquor. This acts as a peripheral vascular dilator, as we say in the cat doctoring profession. Or, in lay terms, gets the blood pounding through the old tubes, relaxing him and loosening his inhibitions.

Should he protest, as he may well do, that he does not care for the beverage, take a firm stand. Ignoring his struggles and screams, force it down his unwilling throat. He will thank you for it after-wards.

7. *Vamp him.* Do not await his arrival in dressing-gown and curlers, with rolling-pin or frying-pan at the ready. Remember that all day he has been subjected to the sight of bronzed, bikini-clad beauties disporting themselves on the canal bank. And he's only human.

Smarten yourself up. Comb your hair. Put your eyelashes on. Put your teeth in. A few generous squirts of *Desert Rapture*. A diaphanous negligee. A ciggie in a long black holder. A seductive, reclining posture on the sofa as he walks through the door.

Ignore his greeting of, 'Have you nowt better to do all day than lie around smoking me fags? Where's me tea?' Stretch out your arms and say, 'Darling . . . Come sit by me and tell me all about it . . . '

The rest is up to you. Don't blame me if, from that crumpled heap of wellies and ganzies, emerges a fiery Casanova, a hot-blooded Latin Lover who makes Sacha Distel and Paul Newman look like Laurel and Hardy.

*　　*　　*

There it is, girls. With just one word of warning. If you work really hard at it, you may find them giving up angling altogether. You'll have them home very weekend. Smashed out of their tiny minds and chasing you all over the house. And you'll *never* get any hoovering done.

Pull your finger out

A song I did *not* learn at my mother's knee was one which went
to the tune of *Way Down South In Dixie*. The singer had done something very anti-social to a woodpecker and, as the song went on to
announce:

> *The woodpecker cried*
> *'God bless my soul!*
> *'Take it out!*
> *'Take it out!*
> *'Take it out!*
> *'Take it out!'*

Ee, me mam would have given me a thick ear if she'd caught me
singing that one.

I was reminded of it, though, by the mention in *Angling Times*
of the technique used by beach ace Fred Williams for quietening
down a big conger.

'Pick it up,' Fred was quoted as saying, 'with your forefinger in
its vent.'

I thought you could get locked up for that.

No, fair do's. I think it's a bit off. I've heard of some funny ways
of quietening eels, but this beats all.

Can you imagine a couple of eels escaping over the side and comparing notes?

'Ooh, it was agony, Adrian. I got yanked up by Peter Collins and
he started bashing hell out of me with a damn great marlin spike.'

'You think *you* had problems, ducky. Fred Williams got me. I
didn't know where to put my face. And I'll swear he never cuts his
nails . . . '

I much prefer the technique Ernie Passmore used on his record
conger: 'I stroked it gently until it relaxed . . . '

Isn't that nice? Dead considerate, that is. A touch of the Great
Lover there. But then Ernie had to spoil it all by picking the poor
little thing up, as it lay there quietly smirking, and chucking it into
the hold.

Still, it was a good start. A bit like the Japanese technique of
stroking those special bulls all through the day and night for about
three years, right up to the time they clobber them. Of course the
clobbering comes as a bit of a surprise, but up until then they're
still giggling and saying (in Japanese) 'Ah, so, cheeky . . . geroff . . . '

I have been working on Ernie's method and I've now got enough variations on it to ensure that no conger ever again need be held down with gaffs, have a finger stuck in a blush-making place, or go to the big *Our Unity* in the sky after being done to death by methods which would have made Attila the Hun throw up in his Christian-skin wellies.

Right, lads. You've got your conger inboard. Now to quieten it.

Stroke it, like Ernie does. Chuck it under the chin. Tickle it under the armpits. Give it a double scotch and a fag.

Sing it an appropriate song. *Aye, Aye, Conger. Eel Meet Again. Congeratulations. Eel, Aye, Addio, You've Won The Cup. Tie Me Conger Eel Down, Sport. Teeth For Two. Fangs For The Memory.*

Tell it a joke:

This conger went into a pub and ordered a pint of bitter.

The barman said, 'Certainly, sir. That'll be 50p.'

The conger paid up, drank his pint, and turned to go.

'Excuse me, sir,' said the barman. 'Don't think I'm being personal, but we don't get many eels in here.'

'With bitter at 50p a pint,' said the conger, 'I'm not bloody surprised.'

Your eel should be all relaxed by now, if not helpless with laughter, and it's time to do the nasties.

You could frighten it to death. Show it a photograph of the wife's mother.

Or you could creep up behind it and give it one swift and fatal blow with a weighted black pudding. Singing, as you did so, this adaptation of another Song of My Childhood:

> *All of a sudden*
> *A dirty black pudden*
> *Came flying through the air.*
> *It hit the conger.*
> *A right old blonger*
> *And knocked it off the chair.*

If you prefer less violent methods, as you doubtless do, you could bore it to death. Tell it your fishing stories. Or your army stories. Or show it the latest statement from the Department of the Environment promising to do something about offshore pollution.

Kill it with kindness. Show it a coloured photograph of a lady eel, starkers. Wave the picture about to get the authentic undulating effect until the lad bursts a blood vessel.

Let it drink six pints of keg bitter straight off, and let the bubbles give it the bends.

Or feed it with the wife's home-made Cornish pasties. And let it burp itself to death.

The last matchman

An end-of-season card in a Teddington Shop Window read:

Left on the bank of the Thames just below
Teddington Lock on Saturday evening, March 9,
a black tin box containing fishing tackle and
upper and lower dentures.

Obviously the poor lad hadn't had much of a day. He'd probably put his choppers in the box to stop himself gnashing his teeth.

But false teeth aren't the half of it. You'd be surprised what get left on the banks in the course of a season. There's tackle of course. Any amount of it. A secondhand dealer could make a fortune by just wandering the banks at night. You get freak losses, like umbrellas, which in a high wind can land miles from where they started. Often with the owner still attached.

But there's other stuff as well. And I bet there's been some right explaining to do about how it got left behind. Trousers, string vests, long johns, chest expanders, trusses, wigs, glass eyes, false beards and wooden legs. ('I'm sorry to come home without my leg, love, but the bailiff told me to hop it.')

And people. Lots of people wandering about. Wives and children, some of them by now widows and orphans, left behind when Dad said, 'Won't be long folks. I'm just popping over to the *Cock and Bottle* to see a man about a frog.'

Angling groupies. The swinging girls who follow the matchmen about, left behind in the rush for the bus after the weigh-in.

Sorry, Missis, what's that? You didn't know there were such things? Ee, I could tell you a few tales about that lot . . .

(By gum, I bet that's stirred things up a bit, here and there.)

And how could any of us forget the most famous lost-and-found angler, Albert (Kamikaze) Clegg? Albert failed to hear the final whistle at the end of a match in Wigan in 1954. Sitting at the end peg, shrouded in fog, he also failed to notice that everybody else had gone home. With his captain's final exhortation ringing in his ears—'We're fishing to the last caster, Albert lad . . . and tek no notice of any barracking by them buggers from Leigh'—Albert fished away steadily for twenty years.

He ignored all appeals from clubmates and police. Indeed, he hurled bricks at anyone who approached too closely. 'Ah'm handing over me rod rest to nobody but Eli Rowbottom, me beloved captain,' he said. And refused to believe that Eli had been run down by a tram in Blackpool the weekend after the match and since then had been unable to leave the cemetery.

Albert was finally captured by an *Angling Times* team, who, under the pretext of photographing his catch of ten thousand tons of roach and bleak, managed to lure him from the bank and lock him in the report station.

There he was visited by his wife who produced the remains of his tea, which had been under the grill for twenty years, and beat him over the head with the remains of two charred black puddings. After that, Albert went quietly to a hero's welcome, and has since been working on his memoirs in the public bar of the *Clog and Trotter*.

So there you are, folks. If you've lost anything—tackle, wellies, long johns, wooden legs, chest expanders, husbands, wives, children, girl friends—don't worry. There's every chance that it will turn up.

Mind you, some of it will have gone off a bit.

Look deep into my eyes

The other week I was hypnotising the cat. Like you do. When it occurred to me that my amazing power over animals could be put to better use.

(Ever tried that, hypnotising the cat? What you do is to wait until it is settled on the back of the settee, and then stare deep into its eyes. You say, 'Daft cat, you are completely in my power. You are going to sleep. A deep . . . deep . . . sleep . . . '

(The cat's eyes cross and eventually close and it sinks rapidly into boboes. It's never been known to fail. Except once, when I put the 'fluence on from too close a range and Liddle Puddy took a chunk out ob by dode.)

Anyway, what I thought was that instead of wasting time on the cat, I could try my hypnotic powers on fish. And transmit them by telepathy, at which I am also a master.

So there I was, down by the canal. At a spot where some record breaking roach can be had. If you know what you're about. Like what I do.

Bait up. Cast out. All systems go. Now for the telepathy.

You are a roach of about 3 lb. in weight. You are very hungry and totally unafraid. You are approaching a maggie of gigantic proportions and irresistible seasoning. You are sucking in the bait. You are—

By gum. That gudgeon must have nipped in a bit smartish. Try again.

You have been shoved aside this time, roach. By big brother. Who weighs all of 4½ lb., and who needs plenty of nourishment. Now, big brother, your little beadies have spotted that delicious anattoed maggie . . . You are moving in for the kill . . . Forgetting your manners and going, 'Slurrrp' . . .

Another bloody gudgeon. Gerroff.

I realise now why the roach are being so shy. It's that 50 lb. carp which is putting them off.

Come here, ol' carp . . . To where the maggie is . . . Parker's here . . . Have no fear . . . Now . . . One . . . two . . . three . . .

If I see another gudgeon, I'll *scream*.

. . . All of which proves that gudgeon are much more receptive to telepathy than 4½ lb. roach and 50 lb. carp. So receptive, so completely in my power, that they elbow the monster fish out of the way to get at the bait first. I wonder if Alwyne Wheeler knows about this?

Meanwhile, perhaps I should keep in practice.

Come here, daft cat. Look deep into my eyes . . . You are going to sleep . . . A deep . . . deep . . . sleep . . .

Monsters and little green men

Some rum fishing stories you read these days.

The former chairman of the National Federation of Fishing Tackle Retailers was attacked by a 60 lb. Celebes ape. And a black leopard cub was found gambolling along the banks of the Medway.

Not so long before, wallabies were going hoppity-hop around a bunch of anglers who were trying to concentrate on the fishing near a safari park. Another angler made all speed backwards when a hippo walked out of the water.

All we were short of was a ghost and then, would you believe, a phantom fisherman disappeared before the very eyes of some flesh-and-blood lads.

None of this surprises me. I've been used to it ever since that parrot walked in front of the car in Hemel Hempstead. But what next?

I'll tell you. With the aid of the Parker Plastic Ball. Going through the cuttings in 1976, I note a sharp increase in the number of Yeti-Bites-Man headlines.

There was the lad at Monton Bridge who was trodden on by an elephant.

'It left me feeling pretty flat,' he told an *Angling Times* reporter.

There were complaints from Pixie's Mere about low-flying pterodactyls swooping on floating crusts.

'It's about time the council stepped in,' said a spokesman for the Anti-Dinosaur Vigilante Committee.

An angler at Redmire had a titanic struggle with what he thought at first was a 60 lb. carp. It turned out to be a 90-ton scaly thing with big teeth and six legs.

'If I'd thought on, I'd have had it set up,' he said. 'But as it was, I took it home for the cat.'

The only bit the cat left, a 12-foot thigh bone, was sent to the Natural History Museum by registered post.

An angler at Claydon Lakes, who put the boot into what he thought was a Golden Labrador eating his butties, discovered his mistake when it chewed his leg off.

'How was I to know it was a lion?' he demanded. 'I'm studying animals in a weekly-part encyclopaedia, but they've only got up to D.'

Perhaps the most unfortunate angler of 1976 was the table-tennis-playing proprietor of a Chinese takeaway shop. He was fishing an ornamental lake in an attempt to meet a rush order for six hi-gois and prawn balls, when he was carried off by a 60-foot gorilla. The gorilla took him up to the belfry of the local church and used him as a clapper to play a triple Bob Major.

How could we forget the headline of the year? :

PING PONG CHING CHONG
IN KING KONG DING DONG

Must go. As I type this, a funny round thing has landed on the lawn. Some little green fellers with BBC 2 aerials sticking out of their heads are walking towards the shed.

Now, what is it you say to these lads? 'Green man speak with forked tongue?' No. Er. 'Lead me to your taker?' No.

Never mind. It'll come to me in a minute. And I'll get me name in t'paper.

Leave 'em laughing when you go

In an earlier, breathtaking instalment, I told how the cow came to fall on me and Cousin Jim from Leeds. But that is not the reason I am scared of cows and bulls and bullocks and heifers and policemen and big gormless things like that.

No. People have whispered behind my front that I am scared of cows because I am a lily-livered, weak-kneed, yellow-bellied, gutless, spineless, snivelling coward. And they are dead right.

But I have now found the answer. The other morning, in a field on the banks of the Thame (the one without the 's') I discovered a technique which got me and Number One Son through a big herd of bullocks without so much as a scratch.

These bullocks had just been put into the field for fattening up, and they were a bit niggly about the whole prospect. They surrounded me and my firstborn and started nudging.

'Gerroff,' I said in my best Eton accent. 'It's not my flaming fault.'

'I've read somewhere', said Number One Son, 'that if you grab them by the tongue, they are absolutely helpless.'

Education is a wonderful thing. He's not just a pretty face, that lad. If he'd read on a bit he might have discovered how you make the bloody things stick their tongues out.

Things were getting really tremble-making when I remembered my old music hall jokes routine, a side-splitting performance guaranteed to empty a four-ale bar in ten seconds flat.

'*I say, I say, I say. My wife has gone to the West Indies.*'

'*Jamaica?*' (I do the voices for the double act as well.)

'*No. She went of her own accord.*'

The three big bullocks who were doing most of the nudging (the biggest of whom I swear hadn't had a proper job done on him) stopped and looked worried. Clouts with the rod rest they could take, but this was something they hadn't bargained for.

'*Waiter, waiter, there's a dead fly in my soup.*'

'*What do you expect for two bob—a dead eagle?*'

Slowly the big lads started backing away.

'*I say, I say, I say. This fish has no nose.*'

'*That fish has no nose? How does it smell?*'

'*Terrible.*'

Suddenly there was space to swing a basket.

'Follow me, son,' I said. 'Pass my khaki trousers and have no fear.'

'*Tell me, bus conductor, do you stop at the Hilton Hotel?*'
'*On my wages, mate? You must be joking.*'
'*Do you like Kipling?*'
'*I don't know. I've never kippled.*'
The bullocks had backed away right on to the old stone bridge. And here was a real snag. We had to cross the bridge and there they were, jammed solid, like the lot that faced Horatio, with the ones at the back crying 'Forward' and the ones at the front crying 'Back'.

(Thought I'd throw that bit in to show that Number One Son is not the only-one with an education.)

'*Yerss . . . I went t'Eton, mate.*'
'*Really? How long were you there?*'
'*Abaht five minutes.*'
The ones at the front were still backing up, but those at the back who couldn't hear, were not budging at all. So I threw in the ultimate deterrent.

'*Ladies and gentlemen. Er . . . gentlemen. Er . . . however you feel about the situation—a little song entitled, 'She Was Only A Fisherman's Daughter, But She Wouldn't Swallow My Line.*'

Hitching up my trousers by the scruff of the fly, to get the authentic Count John McCormack sound, I began:

'*Dere's an ould Oirish mudder*
'*Who's waitin' fer me*
'*In a humble ould cottage*
'*Boi de misty Mersey . . .*'

The bullocks fled, kicking and leaping as if they'd never lost their prospects. And Number One Son and I were free to spend the next four hours proving my theory that the freshwater fish in Britain is extinct.

'That's the secret, lad,' I said as we crossed the bridge. 'Leave 'em laughing when you go.'

*   *   *

Eh, no. It was true, that was . . .

I'll tell you a tale of the Arctic Trail

I've known blokes go to some lengths to catch fish. But night fishing for pike in heavy frost, as practised by Chris Binyon and Roy Thomas of The Lucians Specimen Group, beats all.

To give Chris and Roy something to read while they were thawing out after a particularly chilling trip, I composed this epic poem along the lines of the world renowned *Eskimo Nell*. Old sweats, hoping for a repeat of the 93 verses they used to listen to in the NAAFI, will be disappointed. This version is clean. Near enough.

> When a man grows old
> And his hands grow cold
> And the end of his nose turns blue,
> When he sags in the middle
> Like a one-string fiddle,
> He can tell you a tale or two.
>
> So pull up a chair and stand me a drink
> And a tale to you I'll tell,
> Of Brummagen Chris and Tamworth Roy
> And the Night of the Frozen Hell.
>
> There was frost on the road
> And frost on the trees
> And frost on the trampled grass.
> There was frost on both of Chris's knees
> And right up the Chilcoot Pass.
>
> They had gone out there
> For the fearsome pike,
> The creature bold and bad.
> 'Know what?' said Roy, as they chipped off the ice,
> 'We must be flaming mad.'
>
> 'Have no fear, old friend of mine,'
> Said Chris as his ears hit the turf.
> 'We'll have pike this night
> 'Of such main and might
> 'That the world will know our wurf.'

(What did you expect? Shakespeare or somebody?)

The pike struck once
And the pike struck twice
And the pike struck three times three.
'It's hungry work,' said Tamworth Roy.
'I must have a frozen pea.'

All night they fought with the fearsome fish,
Fought with might and main.
But when morning broke
Neither valiant bloke
Would be the same again.

For their ears were gone
And their faces wan
And their noses all awry.
'I know what I want,' said Tamworth Roy.
'Me too,' said Chris—'to die.'

'At last, at last, I am satisfied.'
Said Roy, as he unhooked the wobblers.
'Do me one last favour, faithful friend—
'Remove that snap from my trousers.'

(There are no naughties in this book.)

They'll tell this tale on the Arctic Trail
Where the nights are sixty below.
Where it's so damn cold
That the deadbait's sold
Wrapped up in a ball of snow.

In the Valley of Death with baited breath
That's where they'll sing it too,
Where the skeletons rattle in a night-long battle
With pike of a ghostly hue.

When a man grows old
And his hands grow cold
And the end of his nose turns blue,
And he freezes all night
In the hope of a bite,
I'd say he was mad—wouldn't you?

The Sludgethorpe Diaries

... being extracts from the diaries and other documents of the Sludgethorpe Waltonians. This from the battered typewriter of Ken Scratcher, ace (and only) reporter of the *Sludgethorpe Echo*.

Vultures for culture

I fear the worst. The town has gone festival daft. Two Thousand Years of Sludgethorpe—I ask you. The place has only been here since the invention of the trip hammer.

But old Harbottle, Chairman of the Waltonians, has had this bee in his bonnet for years. He's not only formed his own Festival Committee at the fishing club, but he's actually got another one going at the Sludgethorpe Chamber of Commerce.

That's how I got the job of judging the entries in the Waltonians' Festival Poetry Competition. Harbottle chatted up my boss, Eli Harmsworth Flongbender, at a Chamber of Commerce booze-up. Old Eli—he inherited the paper from his dad and knows as much about print as I know about brain surgery—came back full of it.

'Culture, m'boy!' he bellowed. (He's as deaf as a post, so he shouts at everybody.) 'The cultural heritage of our dear old town! We'll put this place on the literary map before we're through—and we start with the Waltonians' poetry.

'Double page spread! Give 'em all a prize!' (Eli made a mistake in a stationery order five years ago which left us with four thousand ballpoint pens, so we've never been short of prizes.) 'And tart it up with lots of literary allusions. Mention Shakespeare and ... er ... Kipling and ... er ... all that lot.'

Having run out of poets and being late already for a Licensed Victuallers' jug-up, he cleared off and left me with this slice of Sludgethorpe's living culture.

Look at this, for a start, from McGonogle Harbottle himself:

The Lovesome Gudgeon

A gudgeon is a lovesome thing,
God wot,
Down to its last little speckly spot.
But you need so many for the pot
That really I think I'd rather not.

The Waltonians' match record hasn't been up to much recently, and they're getting a bit sensitive about it. So Horace Harris will be in trouble when the other lads read his piece:

Five Minutes to Go
Rub a dub dub,
Three men and a chub.
One of them strikes
But he's not from our club.

Here's a turnup for the thingy. Bid Eddie Fanshawe. He used to be so busy throwing the Waltonians out of *The Bricklayer's Arms* that he hardly had time to pull a pint. Perhaps being made a life member has addled his brain. Such as it is:

Ruffe Justice
Oft times I lurch
In search
Of a perch.
And I huff
And I puff
When I'm stuck
With a ruffe.

Here's Adrian Paunceworthy, Gay Lib's answer to Brigitte Bardot. How he ever got into the Waltonians is one of the Great Unsolved Mysteries of Our Age. The first time I saw him fishing a match he was wearing rubber gloves to put the maggots on. When I asked him why, he said, 'I'd have thought it was obvious, dear. I've got to *handle* the beastly things.'

Moment Of Truth
When the pike is lurking deep
I'm all hot pepper and mustard.
But when he comes up for a peep
I'm a real old cowardly custard.

Social comment next, from Harry Turner:

Power Boat Rally, Jackson's Clay Pit
There's a cloth-capped, hairy angler
To the north of Foundry Road
And he's more than just a little bit uptight.

The power boats cut his line and ripped his keepnet;
There'll be no more fish for anyone tonight.
So he's waiting till they've stopped their flaming rally;
Till they've stopped their idiot racing and their noise.
He's got one of Jackson's firebricks in his pocket
And he's going to sort the men out from the boys.

I reported the case at the magistrates' court. Harry was fined a tenner and told not to do it again.

The Turners went on holiday to Blackpool. From the sound of this one by young Jason, the grub doesn't seem to have been up to much:

The Landlady's Kipper

Poor little kipper
On my plate.
You've gone and met
A terrible fate.
From the size of you
I'd swear on oath
That smoking really
Stunts your growth.

Here's a nice one. From little Chuck Chansit, the Pakistani member. Gets you right there, doesn't it?

My New Home

I am being very happy here
In this new land of my choosing.
Enjoying the friendship of many nice blokes,
The raining, the fishing and bhoosing.

This one I've saved till last because I still don't believe it. From Jim Kerrigan, the lad who makes that lethal home brew. From the look of this lot, he'd been hard at it:

Ode To A Lickle Duck

Lickle pickle quacky duck,
May I wish you the best of luck?
If instead of 'quack' you warbled 'cuckoo'
I'd have to call you cuckyduckoo.

And people ask me why so many journalists take to the bottle. To kill the pain, on my life, to kill the pain . . .

THE
END
THE END TH
E END THE
END THE

A SELECTION OF BESTSELLERS FROM *SPHERE*

FICTION

A PERFECT STRANGER	Danielle Steel	£1.75 □
MISSING PERSONS	C. Terry Cline Jr	£1.95 □
A GREEN DESIRE	Anton Myrer	£2.50 □
FLOODTIDE	Suzanne Goodwin	£1.95 □
JADE TIGER	Craig Thomas	£2.25 □

FILM & TV TIE-INS

THE YEAR OF LIVING DANGEROUSLY	C. J. Koch	£1.75 □
STAR WARS	George Lucas	£1.75 □
FAME	Leonore Fleischer	£1.75 □
UPSTAIRS, DOWNSTAIRS	John Hawkesworth	£1.50 □

NON-FICTION

A QUESTION OF BALANCE	H.R.H. The Duke of Edinburgh	£1.50 □
THE DEATH OF THE DIAMOND	Edward Jay Epstein	£1.95 □
SUSAN'S STORY	Susan Hampshire	£1.75 □
SECOND LIFE	Stephani Cook	£1.95 □
YOU CAN TEACH YOUR CHILD INTELLIGENCE	David Lewis	£1.95 □

All Sphere books are available at your local bookshop or newsagent, or can be ordered direct from the publisher. Just tick the titles you want and fill in the form below.

Name ____

Address ____

____

Write to Sphere Books, Cash Sales Department, P.O. Box 11, Falmouth, Cornwall TR10 9EN

Please enclose cheque or postal order to the value of the cover price plus:

UK: 45p for the first book, 20p for the second and 14p per copy for each additional book ordered to a maximum charge of £1.63.

OVERSEAS: 75p for the first book and 21p for each additional book.

BFPO & EIRE: 45p for the first book, 20p for the second book plus 14p per copy for the next 7 books, thereafter 8p per book.

Sphere Books reserve the right to show new retail prices on covers which may differ from those previously advertised in the text or elsewhere, and to increase postal rates in accordance with the PO.